paper
sculpture

Over 25 cute and quirky paper mâché projects

JAMES C. COCHRANE

D&C
David and Charles

A DAVID & CHARLES BOOK

David & Charles is an F+W Publications Inc.
company
4700 East Galbraith Road
Cincinnati, OH 45236

First UK edition published 2008

Conceived and produced by Breslich & Foss Ltd,
Unit 2A, Union Court, 20–22 Union Road, London
SW4 6JP

Volume copyright © 2008 by Breslich & Foss Ltd

Photography: Martin Norris
Design: Elizabeth Healey

James C. Cochrane has asserted his right under
the Copyright, Design and Patents Act, 1988, to
be identified as the author of this work.

A catalogue record for this book is available from
the British Library.

ISBN-13: 978-0-7153-2871-2
ISBN-10: 0-7153-2871-9

Printed in China
for David & Charles
Brunel House, Newton Abbot, Devon

Visit our website at
www.davidandcharles.co.uk

David & Charles books are available from all
good bookshops; alternatively you can contact
our Orderline on 0870 9908222 or write to us a
FREEPOST EX2 110, D&C Direct, Newton Abbot,
TQ12 4ZZ (no stamp required UK only).

10 9 8 7 6 5 4 3 2 1

contents

INTRODUCTION

This book is packed with fun ideas as well as hints and tips for making unusual paper sculptures. I first started making pieces from newspaper and glue while studying theatre design at Central Saint Martins School of Art in London. Now I specialise in illustration, as well as in making paper sculptures for shops and galleries around the country and by private commission. My three-dimensional sculptures have become an extension of my illustration work, but have a personality all of their own. Dealing with theatrical props, sets and costumes, I have picked up lots of different techniques using easily accessible and inexpensive materials, many of which I now pass on to you. Once you have mastered the basics you can let your imagination take over!

This book starts with simpler flat wall pieces – for example, the Sequinned Starfish (page 24), the Racing Greyhound (page 38) and the Oriental Dragon (page 64). As well as these, you'll find projects that shape newspaper with masking tape to form three-dimensional pieces to be viewed all around. Using these skills you can make a Pink Piglet, ready to wallow in farmyard mud (page 52), or even a household pet that is very cute and cheap to feed (page 42). Or why not make a Monster and his glamorous girlfriend (page 80)? Towards the end of the book there are projects that use cardboard to build unusual box shapes, a clock face (page 86) and a useful pair of book ends (page 104).

I hope you enjoy all these ideas and progress to personalise and transform them to make your own cardboard and paper masterpieces.

JAMES C. COCHRANE

GETTING STARTED

Before you start to make any of the projects in this book, there are a few tools and materials that you need to get together. All are inexpensive, and most are readily available around the home or from local craft shops and high-street hardware stores.

TOOLS AND MATERIALS

In terms of tools, you will need scissors, a craft knife, a ruler, pens and pencils and paintbrushes. The basic materials are the same for for every project – cardboard (you can simply cut up cardboard boxes), newspaper, 2.5cm (1 in.) wide masking tape, PVA glue, plaster of Paris and white emulsion paint. You will also need strong wire for making hangers for wall-mounted pieces and for strengthening arms, legs and tails, while thin fuse or jewellery wire is useful for whiskers.

BASIC SHAPES

The templates for several of the projects are given at the end of the book (page 116). These are a handy starting point, although you can, of course, draw your own shapes. Use a photocopier to enlarge any template to the size required or use tracing paper to copy it directly.

Other creatures in the book are made without using a template – for example, the Perfect Pooch (page 42) and the March Hare (page 56). For this type of form, first draw the individual elements from reference material such as photographs or your own sketches. The colourful Robot (page 74) is simply constructed from a series of cardboard boxes, which can be short and fat or long and thin, depending on your personal preference.

Some body parts – such as hands, ears and tails – are best drawn freehand, using the photos as a guide, as the exact size and shape will depend on the character of the creature you are creating and on how large you decide to make it.

finished sizes

The sizes of the sculptures are provided as a guide. These are expressed as Height x Width x Depth, and exclude ears and tails unless otherwise stated.

PLASTER OF PARIS MIX

The techniques for building up both wall-mounted and free-standing pieces are demonstrated in full in the Fancy Fish and Night Owl designs (pages 10 and 14). An Important stage is to cover the sculpture in a mix of plaster of Paris, white emulsion paint and PVA glue.

1 Spoon in the necessary amount of plaster of Paris. For a small, wall-mounted piece such as the Sequinned Starfish (page 24), you will need one large spoonful of plaster. For a big, three-dimensional piece such as the March Hare (page 56), you will need four or five large spoonfuls.

2 Add enough cold water to produce a mixture the consistency of double cream.

3 Add approximately 15% PVA glue and 15% white emulsion paint. Mix well and apply to your sculpture with a paintbrush. Wash the brush thoroughly before the plaster sets hard. Leave to dry, overnight.

4 Use a medium-grade sandpaper to smooth away any lumps and bumps. Seal the surface with a coat of white emulsion paint.

DECORATION

Once you have plastered and sanded the basic form, it is ready for decorating. Bright colours and patterns give an individual and jolly character. Add a touch of sparkle with beads, sequins and glitter in contrasting colours.

The exact colours and decorative elements are entirely up to you; I've given some suggestions in the materials lists that accompany each project, but decoration is a very personal thing and what you choose will depend both on what materials you have available and on the style you want to create.

I use acrylic paints, which are available from art shops and large stationers, to decorate my sculptures. They come in many colours, are easy to use, quick to dry and inexpensive.

It is sometimes easier to draw designs, features or patterns onto the emulsioned surface in pencil before you apply the acrylic paint. Many of the projects are shaded in certain places – for instance, around the eyes or face. Use a dilute paint in a darker tone to achieve this effect.

Sparkling finishing touches can be achieved by supergluing or pinning gems, beads or sequins onto the pieces.

Decorative papers, applied with PVA glue, can produce an interesting finish, especially papers with a smaller repeat pattern. Origami paper, cut-up images from magazines or downloads from the Internet are all good sources of material.

tip

When positioning small decorative elements, you may find it easier to place a dab of glue on the sculpture first. Then, pick up the bead or sequin with a pair of tweezers and drop it in place on your design.

VARNISHING

If you want your sculpture to have a shiny surface, the final stage is to apply varnish. Varnishing is also advisable if your sculpture is going to be displayed in a damp environment, such as a bathroom.

Yachting varnish is water resistant, but is spirit based and can yellow in time. You may also need to apply more than one coat. If you are using yachting varnish, make sure you work in a well-ventilated room. I prefer acrylic varnish, which is easier to use, non-toxic and water based.

A coat of varnish gives sculptures an attractive shiny finish, and helps to protect them from damp.

FANCY FISH

MATERIALS

white paper
tracing paper
cardboard
newspaper
masking tape
PVA glue
strong wire for hanger
plaster of Paris
white emulsion paint
sandpaper
polymer clay
acrylic paints: light green,
  dark green, purple, blue,
  gold, white

assorted beads and sequins
  for decoration
superglue
2 black seed beads for
  the eyes

TOOLS

black marker pen
scissors
wire cutters
paintbrushes

FINISHED SIZE:

H9cm x W14cm
(H3½ in. x W5½ in.)

T his colourful fish demonstrates the basic principles of making a flat-backed, wall-mounted piece. These shapes can then be padded out with newspaper to give fatter or flatter pieces. By changing the outline you can make different animals and other, more complex shapes, such as the Glam Gecko on page 27 or the Oriental Dragon on page 64.

1 Collect together reference material for the fish and draw the basic shape on a piece of paper. Alternatively, copy the illustration (*left*) on white paper.

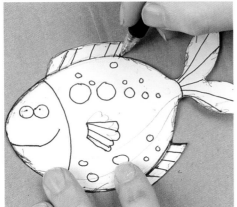

2 Cut out the template and draw around it on cardboard with a black marker pen.

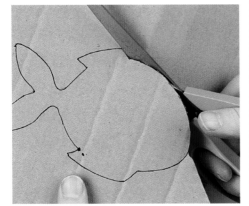

3 Cut out the cardboard fish shape.

4 Tape scrunched-up newspaper onto one side of the cardboard base with masking tape. Make the fish fatter in the middle and flatter on the fins. Continue to tape on newspaper until you are happy with the shape.

5 Tear newspaper into strips about 6 x 2cm (3 x ¾ in.) in size, dip them in PVA glue, and crisscross the fish with the strips. If the glue is too thick, dilute it with a little cold water. Build up two or three layers and leave to dry out. Cover the back of the fish with strips of newspaper for a professional finish.

6 Cut out a small fin shape from cardboard, cover it with strips of newspaper and attach it to the fish body with strips of newspaper dipped in PVA glue.

9 Make eyes out of two small balls of polymer clay. Push in two small glass beads for the pupils. Cook the clay eyes in the oven, following the manufacturer's instructions.

7 Make a hanging loop from strong wire and stick it onto the back of the fish with more strips of newspaper soaked in PVA glue. Leave the fish to dry overnight.

10 Paint the fish with acrylic paint in the colours of your choice and leave it to dry. Glue on the eyes with superglue.

8 When the fish is dry, paint it with a plaster of Paris mix (see page 8) and leave it to dry. When dry, lightly sand the entire surface. Seal the fish with a coat of white emulsion paint and leave it to dry.

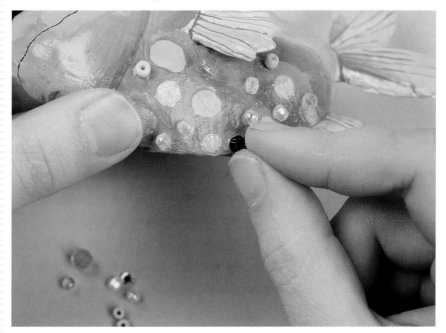

11 Add extra beads and sequins for decoration with superglue.

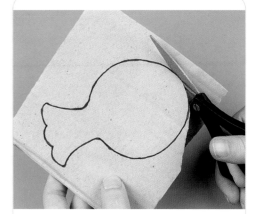

BASIC 3D
PIECE

NIGHT OWL

MATERIALS

template (page 116)
white paper
tracing paper
cardboard
newspaper
masking tape
PVA glue
plaster of Paris
white emulsion paint
sandpaper
acrylic paints: white, black,
   blue, yellow, beige, green,
   orange
superglue
2 black seed beads
   for the eyes

TOOLS

black marker pen
scissors
paintbrushes
pencil

FINISHED SIZE:

H13cm x W11cm x D11cm
(H5 in. x W4½ in. x D4½ in.)

This simple, rounded shape is a good way to progress from the flat-backed shape of the Fancy Fish on page 10 to a three-dimensional form. It uses the same basic techniques, as the owl's body is attached to a flat, cardboard base. The beak and feet are made separately and then joined to the body to make a free-standing piece. The protruding tail feather and oversized claws make it easy for the owl to balance. I've given the bird large painted eyes and decorative oak-leaf camouflage. Why not try your own kind of owl, such as a tall barn owl or a tiny elf owl?

1 Trace the template for the base of the owl from page 116 onto cardboard and cut out.

2 Scrunch up a ball of newspaper for the owl's body and tape it to the base with masking tape. To build up the body shape, add another one or two balls on top of the first one and secure with tape.

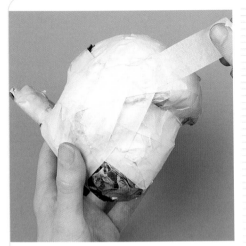

3 Continue to shape the body and tail by building up sections with small areas of scrunched paper taped in place, leaving two shallow dips for the eyes.

5 Continue to cover the owl's body with strips of glued newspaper, adding two ears made of newspaper dipped in PVA, then squeezed out and formed into ear shapes.

7 Place the two beak shapes together, holding at the point. Pad the inside with newpaper, then cover with masking tape. Cover feet and beak with newpaper strips dipped in PVA glue. Leave to dry.

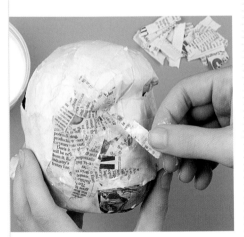

4 Tear newspaper into strips about 6 x 2cm (3 x ¾ in.) in size, dip them in PVA glue and cover the owl's body with them. If the glue is too thick, dilute it with a little cold water.

6 Trace the beak and feet shapes onto cardboard and cut out two of each. Pad one side of the feet with scrunched-up newspaper and masking tape.

8 Attach the feet and beak shapes to the body with newspaper strips dipped in PVA glue. Leave to dry.

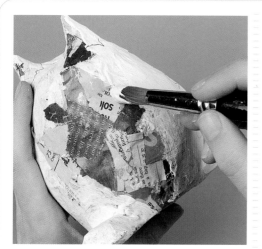

9 Paint the owl with a plaster of Paris mix (see page 8), leave to dry, then lightly sand the entire surface. Paint with a coat of white emulsion paint to seal the body. Leave to dry.

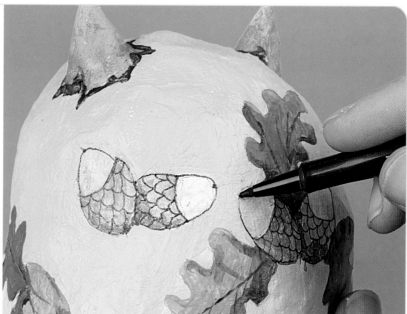

11 Paint the owl and leave it to dry. Outline some of the leaf and acorns with a black pen so that they stand out clearly.

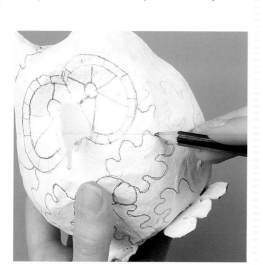

10 Sketch out your own design on paper or copy the owl illustration from page 14. Transfer the owl's features and the oak leaf design onto the body in pencil.

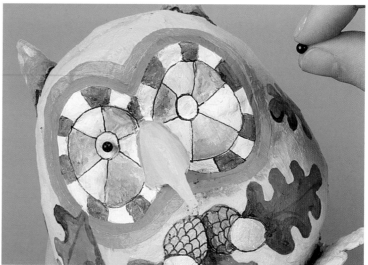

12 Using superglue, attach two black beads for the 'eyes'.

CREATURE FEATURES

Getting the body parts and the expression just right is what gives paper animals their individual characters. Over the next four pages you'll find a basic library of expressions to choose from. Inspiration can be found anywhere: at the zoo, in the park, or while flicking through magazines. And there's no need to restrict yourself to animals: study the faces of children and adults for unusual or comical expressions that can help bring your paper sculptures to life.

CATS

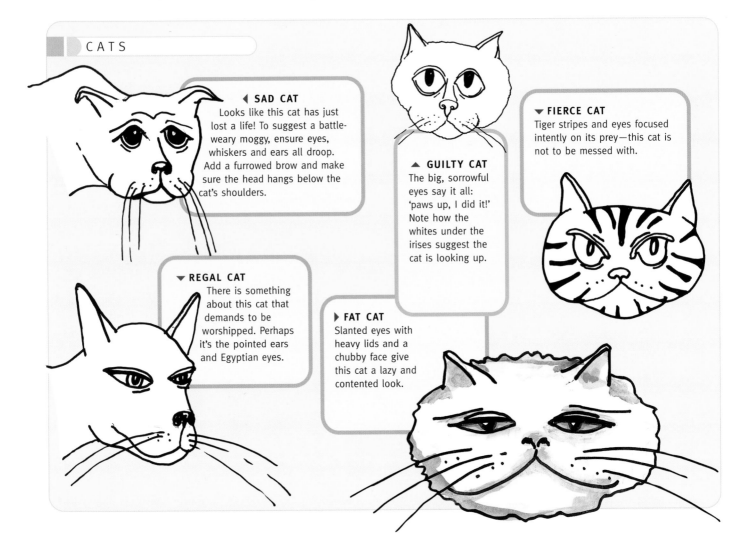

◄ **SAD CAT**
Looks like this cat has just lost a life! To suggest a battle-weary moggy, ensure eyes, whiskers and ears all droop. Add a furrowed brow and make sure the head hangs below the cat's shoulders.

▲ **GUILTY CAT**
The big, sorrowful eyes say it all: 'paws up, I did it!' Note how the whites under the irises suggest the cat is looking up.

▼ **FIERCE CAT**
Tiger stripes and eyes focused intently on its prey—this cat is not to be messed with.

▼ **REGAL CAT**
There is something about this cat that demands to be worshipped. Perhaps it's the pointed ears and Egyptian eyes.

▶ **FAT CAT**
Slanted eyes with heavy lids and a chubby face give this cat a lazy and contented look.

DOGS

▶ **LAP DOG**
With the features taking up just a quarter of the face, this dog becomes a giant ball of fluff. The cross-eyed pupils suggest the dog might be a little dazed from all the constant grooming.

▶ **CUTE SPANIEL**
An adorable scamp with a heart-shape face, enormous love-me eyes and big fluffy ears. Note the minimal use of white in the eyes.

▼ **SNOOTY POODLE**
An upturned nose, a satisfied smirk, and a fancy coiffure suggest a vain and snobbish mutt. Note how its eyes are shut to the horrors of the world.

▲ **BOXER DOG**
What a bruiser! The black eye perfectly sums up the nature of this pugnacious mutt.

▶ **GREAT DANE**
Heavy jowls and hooded lids give this hound a serious demeanour.

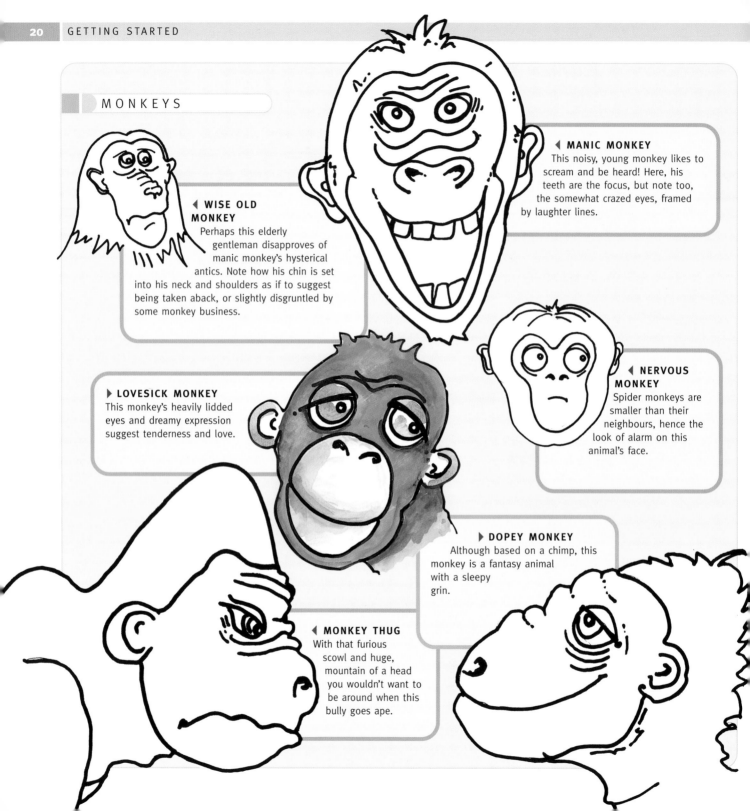

MONKEYS

◀ **WISE OLD MONKEY**
Perhaps this elderly gentleman disapproves of manic monkey's hysterical antics. Note how his chin is set into his neck and shoulders as if to suggest being taken aback, or slightly disgruntled by some monkey business.

◀ **MANIC MONKEY**
This noisy, young monkey likes to scream and be heard! Here, his teeth are the focus, but note too, the somewhat crazed eyes, framed by laughter lines.

▶ **LOVESICK MONKEY**
This monkey's heavily lidded eyes and dreamy expression suggest tenderness and love.

◀ **NERVOUS MONKEY**
Spider monkeys are smaller than their neighbours, hence the look of alarm on this animal's face.

▶ **DOPEY MONKEY**
Although based on a chimp, this monkey is a fantasy animal with a sleepy grin.

◀ **MONKEY THUG**
With that furious scowl and huge, mountain of a head you wouldn't want to be around when this bully goes ape.

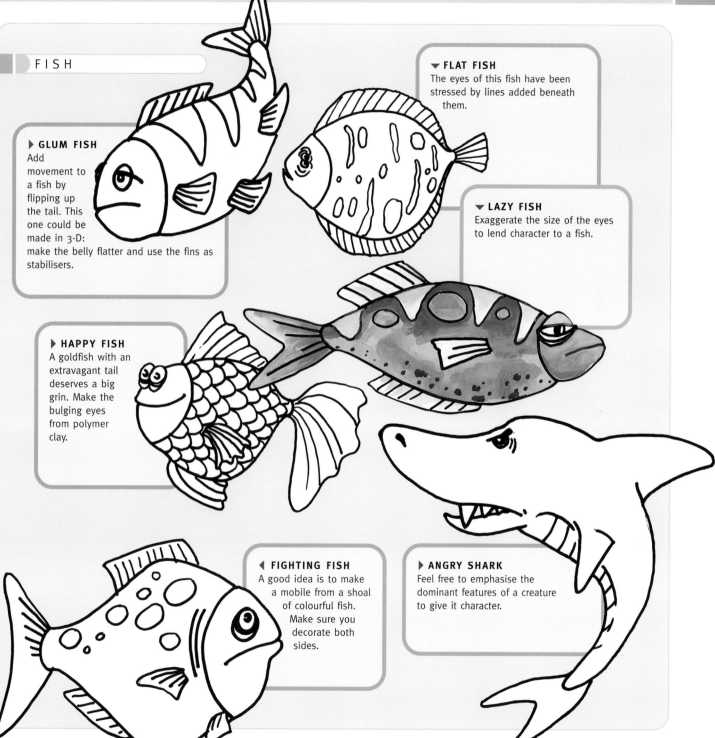

FISH

▶ GLUM FISH
Add movement to a fish by flipping up the tail. This one could be made in 3-D: make the belly flatter and use the fins as stabilisers.

▼ FLAT FISH
The eyes of this fish have been stressed by lines added beneath them.

▼ LAZY FISH
Exaggerate the size of the eyes to lend character to a fish.

▶ HAPPY FISH
A goldfish with an extravagant tail deserves a big grin. Make the bulging eyes from polymer clay.

◀ FIGHTING FISH
A good idea is to make a mobile from a shoal of colourful fish. Make sure you decorate both sides.

▶ ANGRY SHARK
Feel free to emphasise the dominant features of a creature to give it character.

the projects

SKILL LEVEL
★

SEQUINNED STARFISH

MATERIALS

white paper
tracing paper
cardboard
newspaper
masking tape
PVA glue
assorted beads for texture
  and decoration
superglue
plaster of Paris
white emulsion paint
sandpaper
acrylic paints:
  white, orange,
  yellow, red, blue
strong wire for hanger

TOOLS

black marker pen
scissors
paintbrushes
wire cutters

FINISHED SIZE:

H15cm x W15cm
(H6 in. x W6 in.)

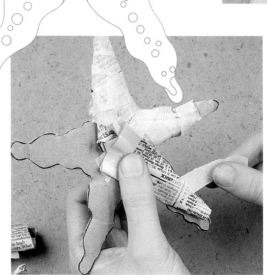

Make your own colourful starfish to brighten up a bathroom wall. Ours are decorated with an assortment of sequins and beads. To give your starfish character, make eyes from polymer clay and two black beads. Bake the clay in the oven following the manufacturer's instructions and glue the beads on top before attaching to the starfish.

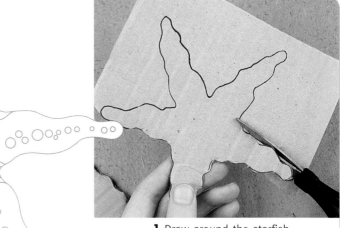

1 Draw around the starfish illustration to make a template. Trace the template onto cardboard and cut it out.

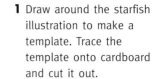

2 Pad one side of the starfish shape with scrunched-up newspaper secured with masking tape.

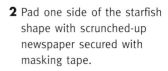

3 Cover the padded-out side of the starfish with strips of newspaper dipped in PVA glue and leave to dry. When dry, use superglue to stick on beads of different sizes to create a knobbly texture.

4 Paint both sides of the starfish with a plaster of Paris mix (see page 8), leave to dry, then lightly sand the surface. Seal the starfish with a coat of white emulsion paint and leave to dry.

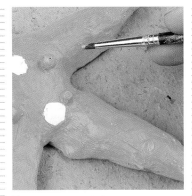

5 Paint the starfish in an orange base colour. Paint a darker tone of orange around the edges of the legs to create some shading. Leave some spots white.

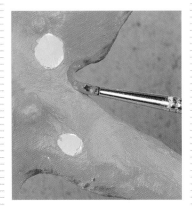

6 Add spots to the white areas of the body in bright, contrasting colours. Add more shading around the legs. Leave to dry.

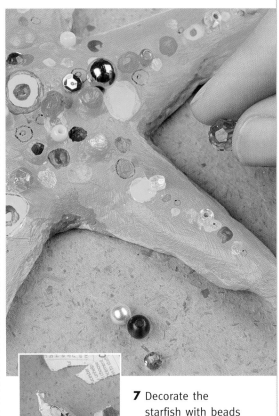

7 Decorate the starfish with beads and sequins. Make a hanger from strong wire and attach it to the back of the starfish with strips of newspaper dipped in PVA glue.

GLAM GECKO

MATERIALS

white paper
tracing paper
cardboard
newspaper
masking tape
PVA glue
strong wire for hanger
plaster of Paris
white emulsion paint
sandpaper
acrylic paints: red, orange,
    yellow, blue, green, white,
    black, silver
scraps of patterned paper
flat-backed gemstones
    (including one for the eye)
sequins

TOOLS

black marker pen
scissors
pencil
wire cutters
paintbrushes

FINISHED SIZE:

H25cm x W13cm
(H10 in. x W5 in.)

In the wild, geckos can be found hiding under stones or in dark crevices. This gecko, however, definitely wants to be seen and is decorated with bright papers as well as with jewels and painted shapes. Add a wire hanger to the back and the gecko will be able to hang on a wall just like the real thing!

1 Draw around the body and the legs of the gecko to create three templates. Trace around them onto cardboard and cut out. Pad one side of the body and the two leg shapes with scrunched-up newspaper secured with masking tape. Cover the separate pieces with strips of newspaper dipped in PVA glue and leave to dry.

2 Attach the legs to the gecko's body with strips of newspaper dipped in PVA glue. Make a wire hanger and attach it to the back of the gecko with more glued newspaper.

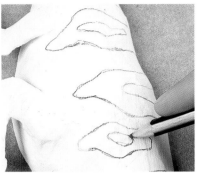

3 Paint the gecko with a plaster of Paris mix (see page 8), leave to dry, then sand. Seal the surface with a coat of white emulsion paint and leave to dry. Draw in the gecko's markings with pencil.

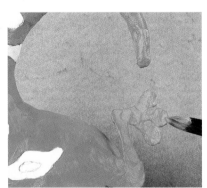

4 Paint the body red, leaving some markings white.

5 Add orange shading around the legs.

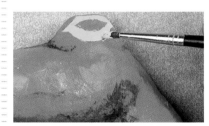

6 Paint in more of the gecko's markings on the body and around the eye.

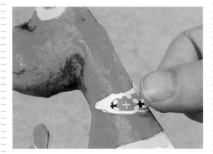

7 Glue scraps of patterned papers onto the remaining white areas of the body. Use brightly coloured paper with a small-scale pattern that won't overpower the design.

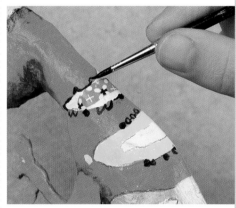

8 Using a fine paintbrush, decorate the body with black paint.

9 Decorate the body with sequins and gemstones, including one for the eye.

CAT'S WHISKERS

This head is based on a Siamese cat, so it has large, pointed ears and an elegant face. To make a tabby cat, make the head round with smaller ears. The head shape is made from a simple cut-out and the ears are added at a later stage. Paint in the markings to fit the breed – and don't forget to capture the expression (see Creature Features on page 18).

MATERIALS

white paper	pin
tracing paper	coloured craft wire
cardboard	superglue
newspaper	
masking tape	**TOOLS**
PVA glue	black marker pen
polymer clay	scissors
strong wire for hanger	wire cutters
plaster of Paris	paintbrushes
white emulsion paint	pencil
sandpaper	
acrylic paints: white,	**FINISHED SIZE:**
black, blue, brown,	H9cm x W 10cm
pink	(H3½ in. x 4 in.)
	ears L5cm (2 in.) each

1 Draw around the cat head illustration (excluding the ears) to make a template. Trace it onto cardboard and cut out. Pad one side with scrunched-up newspaper and secure with masking tape. Build up a central ridge for a nose and add two cheeks.

2 To make the ears, sandwich together six layers of newspaper with PVA glue and leave to dry.

3 Draw two ear shapes on the sandwiched layers and cut them out. Cut two or three snips in the bottom of each ear with scissors to make a tab.

4 Cover the cat's head with strips of newspaper dipped in PVA glue. Bend the ears into shape and secure the tabs with more strips of glued newspaper.

5 Make a nose from polymer clay and bake, following the manufacturer's instructions. When cool, glue it in position on the cat's face using PVA glue. Make a wire hanger and attach it to the back of the head with more strips of newspaper.

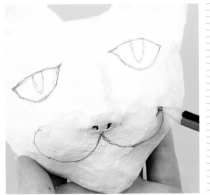

6 Paint the cat's head with a plaster of Paris mix (see page 8), leave to dry, then sand. Seal the cat's head with a coat of white emulsion paint and leave to dry. Draw in the features with pencil.

7 Paint in the cat's markings and eyes. Paint the irises a darker shade at the top. Add in an oval pupil and outline the eyes with a thin black line. Paint a tiny white dot in the corner of each pupil to give the cat a lifelike expression.

8 Cut six 10–12 cm (4–5 in.) lengths of coloured craft wire for the cat's whiskers. Make three holes on each side of the face with a pin, then superglue a piece of wire into each hole.

DAIRY COW

MATERIALS

white paper
tracing paper
cardboard
newspaper
masking tape
PVA glue
strong wire for hanger
plaster of Paris
white emulsion paint
sandpaper
acrylic paints: pink
 (two shades), black,
 grey, beige, brown
small flower decoration
superglue

TOOLS

scissors
paintbrushes
wire cutters
pencil
pin

FINISHED SIZE:

H14cm x W9cm
(H5½ in. x W3½ in.)
ears L5.5cm (2¼ in.) each

This Friesian cow is a champion milk producer with classic black-and-white markings. When you paint a head like this, think about where it will hang on the wall and adapt the feature placement and expression accordingly. If the cow will be looking down at you from near the ceiling, the eyes should be slightly lowered, whereas if it will be displayed at eye level she should gaze directly at you. By searching out suitable reference material, you could easily adapt this design to make a Highland cow with long curly horns and a ring through its nose.

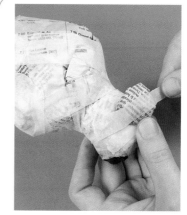

1 Draw around the cow head illustration (excluding the ears and horns) to make a template. Pad one side with scrunched-up newspaper and secure with masking tape. Build up the muzzle with flattened balls of newspaper.

2 Make a pair of ears following the method given on pages 30 to 32.

3 Cover the head with strips of newspaper dipped in PVA glue. Attach the ears with more strips of newspaper. To make horns, cut out two horn shapes from cardboard, cover them with strips of newspaper dipped in PVA glue, then fix them to the top of the head. Make a wire hanger and attach it to the back with more strips of glued newspaper.

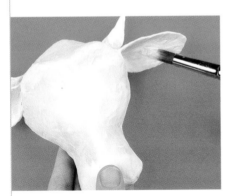

4 Paint the whole head with a plaster of Paris mix (see page 8), leave to dry, then lightly sand. Seal with a coat of white emulsion paint and leave to dry. Paint the insides of the ears in two shades of pink.

5 Draw in the eyes with pencil. Spatter the head with tiny flecks of black paint and start to paint in the eyes.

6 Add shading to the cow's face in beige, grey and brown paint. Paint darker colours under the ears and around the eyes to help them stand out.

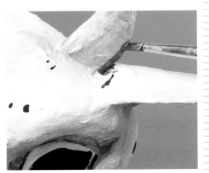

7 Paint the horns in beige, with brown shading around the base.

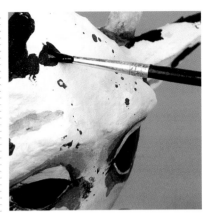

8 Paint the large black markings on the head.

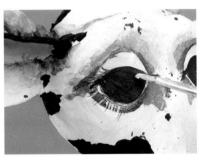

9 Using a fine paintbrush, paint in the eyelashes and add a white spot in the corner of each eye.

10 Make a hole in the muzzle with a pin and glue in a paper flower.

SKILL LEVEL
★★

MORE FOR THE WALL

Why not try one of these three heads or invent an idea of your own? Trace around the basic head shape (excluding the ears) of the cat or the cow on pages 30 and 33, depending on whether the animal you want to recreate has a round or a long face. Remember to attach a loop of wire to the back of the heads with strips of newspaper so you can display them.

 ## MONTY THE RHINOCEROS

This rhinoceros has a flat brow with two heavy eyelids and two medium black beads for eyes. It has large ears on the top of the head and two small ridges to form nostrils. It is painted in a medium grey with beige and light blue rings around his eyes. Don't forget to add a magnificent horn to the end of his snout! Make it by roughly shaping a cone of newspaper and wrapping it with tape.

 ## EXOTIC TIGER

The tiger head is very similar to the cat on page 30, but with shaggy triangular cut-outs included on the cardboard template around the neck. First paint it orange with a white muzzle, then add a lighter shade of orange across the forehead. The eyes are mostly yellow, with a darker ring and a small amount of white showing inside a heavy black outline.

 ## CAPTAIN SKULL

Captain Skull's eyes are made from polymer clay and glass beads, set in two dips created by pressing into the head with your thumb. The black features, gold tooth and red glasses are all painted. Complete the skull with a selection of gems and a pair of glamourous spectacles.

RACING GREYHOUND

I gave this graceful greyhound an elongated, curved body to emphasise its movement and speed. You could make six greyhounds and stage a race around the room! Give them brightly coloured jackets with their numbers on or add the dogs' names in glitter paint.

MATERIALS
white paper
cardboard
strong wire for tail and hanger
newspaper
masking tape
PVA glue
polymer clay
plaster of Paris
white emulsion paint
sandpaper
acrylic paints: black, white, pink, red, blue
superglue
1 x 3cm (½ x 1¼ in.) strip of leather or felt

TOOLS
black marker pen
scissors
wire cutters
paintbrushes
pencil

FINISHED SIZE:
H4-5cm x W46cm
(H2 in. x W18 in.)

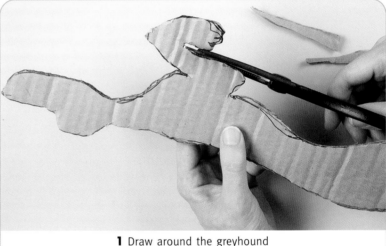

1 Draw around the greyhound illustration to make a template. Transfer the shape onto cardboard and cut it out.

2 To strengthen the tail, tape a piece of wire along its length.

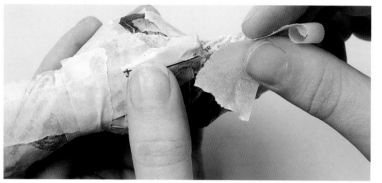

5 Attach the ear and eyebrow to the head with masking tape. Make a wire hanger and attach it to the back of the head with more strips of glued newspaper.

3 Pad one side of the body and the head with scrunched up-newspaper secured with masking tape. Make an ear following the method given on pages 30 to 32. Set aside for use in Step 5.

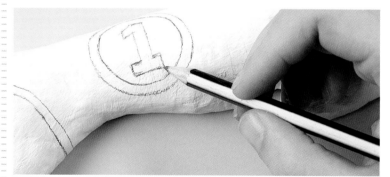

4 Shape the head, making it rounder and fuller than the neck and body. Make an eyebrow from a very small roll of newspaper bent into an arch.

6 Cover the greyhound with strips of newspaper dipped in PVA glue. Make a small nose from polymer clay, and bake in the oven following the manufacturer's instructions. When cool, glue it to the head. Leave to dry. Paint the greyhound with a plaster of Paris mix (see page 8), leave to dry, then sand. Seal the greyhound with a coat of white emulsion paint and leave to dry. Draw in the jacket markings and face with pencil.

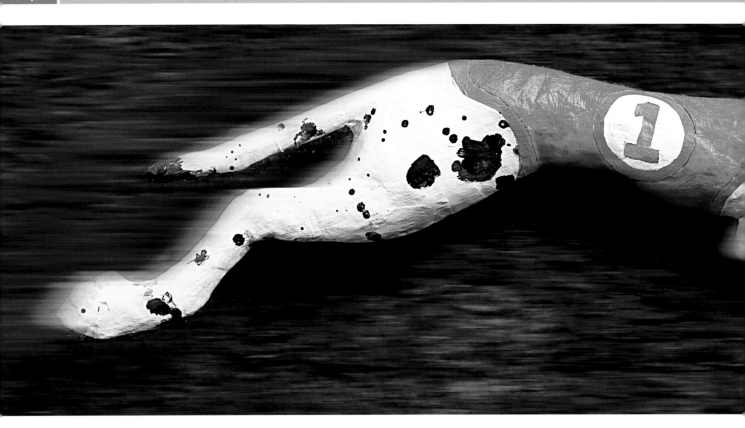

6 Paint the nose in black, then add a fine line for a mouth and spots for whiskers. Shade around the muzzle in pink and around the eye in brown.

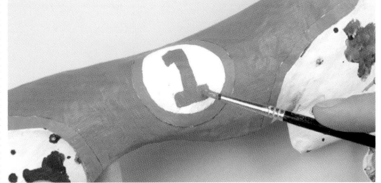

7 Paint in the jacket and add the greyhound's name or number.

8 Using superglue, glue on a strip of leather or felt to form a collar.

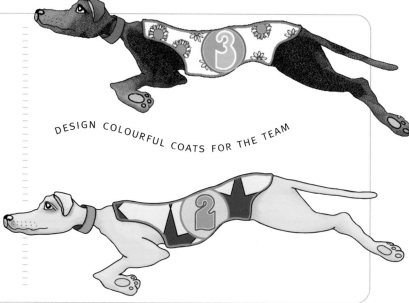

DESIGN COLOURFUL COATS FOR THE TEAM

PERFECT POOCH

Dogs can be made in various positions: standing, sitting or lying curled up. Details such as the ears can show the mood and character of the dog, and painting a hairy coat helps to depict the breed. Creature Features on page 18 should inspire you to find just the right expression for your dog.

Instead of being attached to a flat, cardboard base, this pooch's body, legs, paws, neck, head and tail are all made separately and then joined together. Long limbs and tails may need a wire frame in their construction to give added support, especially while they are drying.

1 Use photographs of your dog taken from various angles to work out the basic body shapes required. Make a sketch of these to follow as you work.

MATERIALS
white paper
newspaper
masking tape
cardboard
PVA glue
polymer clay
plaster of Paris
white emulsion paint
sandpaper
acrylic paints the
   colour of your
   dog's coat

TOOLS
black marker pen
scissors
paintbrushes

FINISHED SIZE:
H33cm x W15cm x D23cm
(H13 in. x W6 in. x D9 in.)

BODY PARTS
you will need...

Body   Head and   Thigh x 2   Front   Hind legs x 2
        neck   legs x 2   Tail

2 Start shaping the main body piece by scrunching up sheets of newspaper.

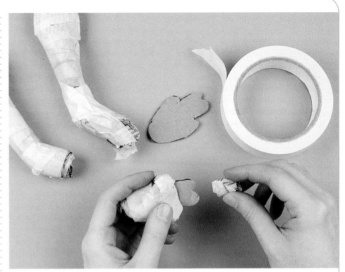

3 Wrap masking tape around the scrunched-up newspaper.

4 Add more scrunched-up newspaper to build up the body, taping the pieces together.

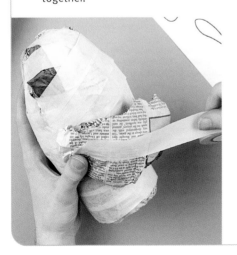

5 When you are happy with the body shape, wrap tape all around it to hold the sections firmly in place.

6 Make the upper part of the front legs in the same way as the body. Make the paws and tail by cutting shapes from card and padding them with newspaper and masking tape. Attach the paws to the front legs. Make the hind legs in the same way.

7 Build the head in two sections: one for the crown and one for the muzzle. Make the neck from a tube of five or six sheets of newspaper secured with masking tape.

8 Join the head and neck sections together with plenty of masking tape.

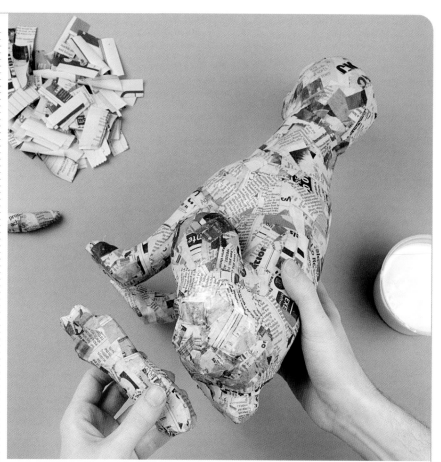

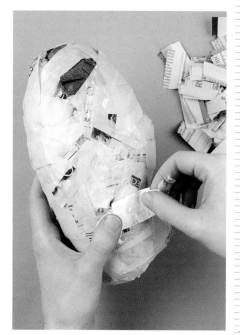

9 Cover each individual body part with strips of newspaper dipped in PVA glue. Leave to dry overnight.

10 Join the body, head and limbs together with more strips of newspaper dipped in PVA glue.

11 Make a pair of ears following the method given on pages 30 to 32. Bend them around to form the right shape for your breed.

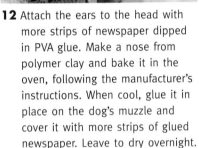

13 Paint the entire body with a plaster of Paris mix (see page 8). When this is dry, sandpaper the surface to give it a smooth finish.

12 Attach the ears to the head with more strips of newspaper dipped in PVA glue. Make a nose from polymer clay and bake it in the oven, following the manufacturer's instructions. When cool, glue it in place on the dog's muzzle and cover it with more strips of glued newspaper. Leave to dry overnight.

DOG ANGLES

WHEN FINISHED YOU WILL HAVE A FULLY, THREE-DIMENSIONAL DOG: THE ONLY THING MISSING WILL BE THE BARK! WE'VE PROVIDED SIDES, BACK AND FRONT VIEWS TO SHOW HOW OUR DOG LOOKS FROM EVERY ANGLE.

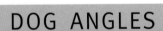

15 Paint on the larger markings where you want them.

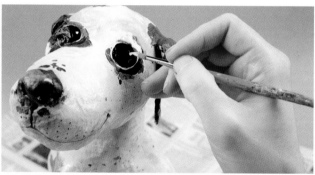

14 Paint the dog with a coat of white emulsion. When dry, paint the basic coat colour of the dog with acrylic paint. Spatter with a darker colour to make natural-looking spots.

16 Paint the face details with a fine paintbrush and leave to dry.

QUEEN'S CORGI

Queen Elizabeth II has always kept her own corgis and here is one for you to recreate. This royal creature is even sporting one of Elizabeth's spare crowns. You can change the breed of the dog by varying its ear shape and fur colour. Alternatively, this idea can easily by adapted to make a Victorian-style moose head hunting trophy with oversized antlers instead of a crown!

MATERIALS

template (page 117)
tracing paper
white paper
cardboard
newspaper
masking tape
PVA glue
superglue
polymer clay
plaster of Paris
white emulsion paint
sandpaper
acrylic paints: gold, sand, white, brown, black, pink
strong wire for hanger
8 x 8cm (3½ x 3½ in.) piece of velvet, satin or silk
assorted glass beads and sequins for decoration
10cm (4 in.) length of pearl braiding for 'necklace'
1 x 3cm (½ x 1¼ in.) strip of leather

TOOLS

black marker pen
scissors
wire cutters
paintbrushes

FINISHED SIZE:

H18cm x W13cm x D10cm
(H7 in. x W5 in. x D4 in.)

1 Using the template on page 117, trace the corgi's head and crown onto cardboard and cut out.

2 Pad the head with scrunched-up newspaper and wrap with masking tape. Form two eye sockets by pushing the paper in with your thumbs on either side of the snout and build up the brow. Cover the crown with a thin layer of newspaper and tape.

3 Make a muzzle from scrunched-up newspaper covered in masking tape. Fix it to the front of the dog's head with more tape.

4 Make a pair of ears following the method given on pages 30 to 32. Make a nose from polymer clay and bake, following the manufacturer's instructions. When cool, fix it in place with strips of glued newspaper. Paint the head with a plaster of Paris mix (see page 8), leave to dry, then sand. Make a wire hanger and attach it to the back of the head with more glued newspaper.

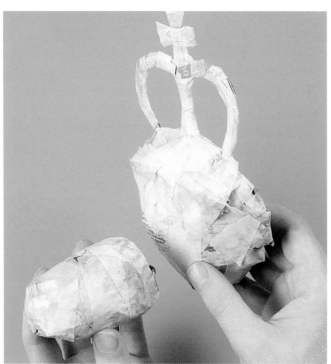

5 Seal with a coat of white emulsion paint and leave to dry. Draw in the corgi's features in pencil and paint the crown gold.

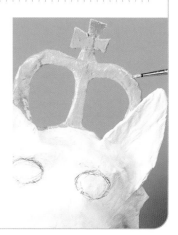

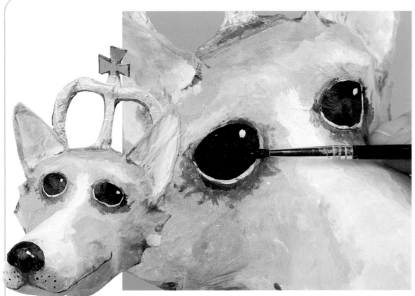

8 Stick the fabric to the crown, folding it slightly in places to create wrinkles in the fabric.

6 Paint the dog's head in a sand colour with a white muzzle. Add brown shading around the eyes, at the base of the ears and around the edge of the head. Paint the nose and eyes in black and the ears in tones of pink.

7 Cut a piece of purple velvet, satin or silk that is slightly wider than the crown and cover the reverse of the crown with glue.

9 Decorate the crown with a selection of flat-backed gems and sequins. Drape a string of pearls around the head.

PINK PIGLET

MATERIALS

cardboard
newspaper
masking tape
PVA adhesive
polymer clay
plaster of Paris
white emulsion paint
sandpaper
acrylic paints: white,
    black, brown and shades
    of red and pink
string

superglue
2 black beads

TOOLS

scissors
paintbrushes
pencil
craft knife

FINISHED SIZE:

H23cm x W15cm x D18cm
(H9 in. x W6 in. x D7 in.)
tail L15cm (6 in.)

BODY PARTS
you will need...

| Body | Head and snout | Ears | Front legs x 2 | Hind legs x 2 |

This little piggy would look cute sitting on a mantelpiece of windowsill, waving at passers-by. I gave the piglet an oversized bottom and stretched-out hind legs to stop it toppling over. The piglet is painted in a bold, simple style, but given more character by a generous spattering of 'mud'.

1 Make a sketch of the basic body shapes to follow as you work. Draw a base for the pig's bottom and hind legs on cardboard and cut it out. Build up the body on top of the base with scrunched-up newspaper wrapped with masking tape. Leave the two hind-leg sections of the cardboard base unwrapped, as shown.

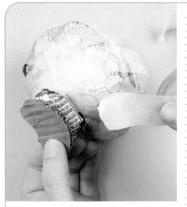

2 Make a head shape from scrunched-up newspaper wrapped in masking tape. Make a snout with a flat end by taping more scrunched-up newspaper to a disc of cardboard.

3 Make four legs by scrunching newspaper into sausages with 'V' shapes at the ends for trotters and wrapping them with masking tape. Cover the body and legs in a layer of newspaper strips dipped in PVA glue.

4 Attach the two hind legs to the unwrapped sections of the base from Step 1. Secure them to the cardboard with strips of paper dipped in PVA glue. Place the head in position and fix it to the body, along with the two remaining legs.

5 Make a pair of ears following the method given on pages 30 to 32, but bend them into a 'piggy' shape. Attach them to the body with strips of glued newspaper and leave to dry. Paint the piglet with a plaster of Paris mix (see page 8), leave to dry, then sand.

6 Seal the piglet with a coat of white emulsion paint and leave to dry. Paint the body in a pale pink base colour.

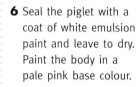
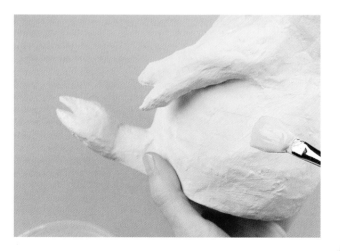

7 Paint the ears in a darker shade of pink, then draw in the facial features with a pencil.

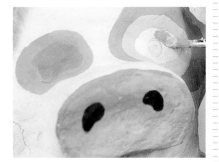

8 Paint the end of the snout in a darker shade of pink, then paint the nostrils in dark brown. Paint rings of different shades of pink around the eyes.

9 Paint the trotters dark brown. Spatter the piglet's body with brown paint for a muddy effect and paint in the belly button.

10 To make the tail, dip string in PVA glue, coil it around the end of a large paintbrush and leave to dry. When dry, remove it from the paintbrush and paint it pink. Make a small hole in the body with a craft knife and glue the end of the tail into the hole.

11 Superglue two black beads in place for the eyes.

PIG ANGLES

THIS PROJECT DEMONSTRATES HOW ATTRACTIVE A FLAT, CARTOON STYLE OF DECORATION CAN BE. THE PIGLET IS GIVEN CHARACTER THROUGH THE SPATTERED PAINT EFFECT AND THE FOLDED-OVER EARS.

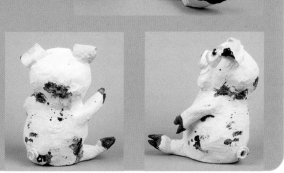

MARCH HARE

This mystic March hare gazes longingly at the full moon. The eyes are placed so the hare appears to survey the countryside with its bright orange eyes, ready to make a run for cover. I've given it extra-long ears and whiskers and an electric-blue fur coat, but you could use more realistic colouring if you prefer.

MATERIALS

white paper
newspaper
masking tape
cardboard
PVA glue
polymer clay
plaster of Paris
white emulsion paint
sandpaper
acrylic paints: medium blue,
    white, pink, orange, black,
    brown
fine wire for necklace and
    whiskers
selection of beads and
    gemstones
cotton wool ball
superglue

TOOLS

black marker pen
scissors
paintbrushes
pin

FINISHED SIZE:

H28cm x W15cm x D18cm
(H11 in. x W6 in. x D7 in.)
ears L18cm (7 in.) each

BODY PARTS

you will need...

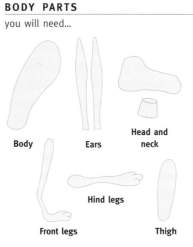

Body   Ears   Head and
                            neck

Hind legs

Front legs   Thigh

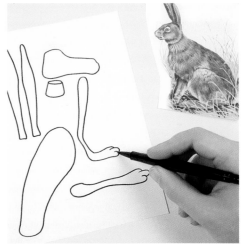

1 Make a sketch of the basic body shapes to follow as you work.

2 Wrap strips of masking tape around scrunched-up pieces of newspaper to build up a body form. Mould the shape by joining up several pieces.

3 Make the head in the same way and build up the cheeks with balls of newspaper held in place with masking tape. Create eye sockets by building up the brow above them with small rolls of newspaper.

4 Make a neck from six sheets of newspaper rolled into a tube and secured with masking tape. Make four long legs and paws using the method given on page 44. Cover all the pieces with newspaper strips dipped in PVA glue.

5 Fix the legs to the body with strips of newspaper dipped in PVA glue.

6 Make a pair of ears following the method given on pages 30 to 32, but make them very long and thin. Join the head and neck sections together with plenty of masking tape and cover the joins with strips of glued newspaper. Attach the ears. Make a small nose from polymer clay and bake, following the manufacturer's instructions. When cooks, glue it in place. Paint the hare with a plaster of Paris mix (see page 8), leave to dry, then sand.

7 Seal the hare with a coat of white emulsion paint and leave to dry. Paint the hare's body in a base coat of medium blue and the paws, stomach and snout in white.

8 Paint the inside of the ears pink and the eyes orange with black pupils. Add a small rim of white around the outside.

9 Paint the nose black and the snout pink, then use a fine paintbrush to add black dots for whiskers.

10 Make a necklace by threading assorted coloured beads onto fine wire and fixing it around the hare's neck. Using a pin, make six holes in the hare's cheeks and superglue long pieces of fine wire into the holes to make whiskers.

11 To make the tail, dip a piece of cotton wool in PVA glue. When it is dry, stick it in place with superglue.

HARE ANGLES

TO MAKE A MOON-GAZING HARE LIKE THIS ONE, PAINT THE EYES SO THAT THE CREATURE LOOKS UPWARDS. A WHITE DOT AT THE TOP RIGHT-HAND CORNER OF EACH PUPIL AIDS THE EFFECT. THE LARGE LIMBS HELP THE SCULPTURE TO REMAIN STABLE.

GREY GORILLA

Gorilla are one of the closest species to mankind. They share flexible hands and fingers and are able to make wonderful facial expressions. The long arms and huge hands are designed to keep the gorilla stable. The body, arms and hand pieces a made separately before being joined otogether to create a balanced and secure sculpture.

MATERIALS
white paper
newspaper
masking tape
strong wire
cardboard
PVA glue
polymer clay
plaster of Paris
white emulsion paint
sandpaper
acrylic paints: pink, grey,
    mid-brown, dark
    brown, white, black
polymer clay
superglue

TOOLS
pencil
wire cutters
scissors
paintbrushes

FINISHED SIZE:
H19cm x W28cm x D8cm
(H7½ in. x W1 in. x D3 in.)

BODY PARTS
you will need...

Head   Body

Feet   Hand   Arms

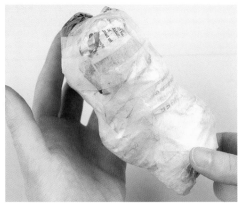

1 Make a sketch of the basic body shapes to follow as you work. Wrap scrunched-up pieces of newspaper with pieces of masking tape to build up a body form.

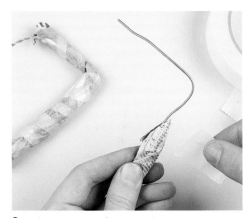

2 Make two arms by wrapping newspaper around lengths of strong wire bent to shape. Fix with pieces of masking tape. Leave a short length of wire unwrapped at each end to use when attaching the arms to the body and hands.

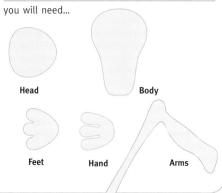

3 Cut out two hand shapes from cardboard, pad both sides with scrunched-up newspaper and secure with masking tape. Push the wire from the ends of the arms into the hands and tape securely to create wrists. Bend the fingers into shape.

5 Make two nipples and two ears from polymer clay and bake, following the manufacturer's instructions. When cool, fix them in place with PVA glue. Leave the gorilla to dry out.

4 Wrap scrunched-up newspaper with pieces of masking tape to build up a head. Build up an enlarged jaw and create eye sockets by building up the brow with rolls of newspaper secured with masking tape. Cut out two feet shapes from cardboard and pad one side. Cover the body parts with newspaper strips dipped in PVA glue. Join the sections together with more strips of glued newspaper.

GORILLA ANGLES

THIS CHEEKY GORILLA IS A DELIGHT FROM EVERY ANGLE. YOU MAY NEED TO ADJUST THE POSITION OF THE ARMS IN STEP 4 FOR BALANCE BEFORE FIXING THEM IN POSITION.

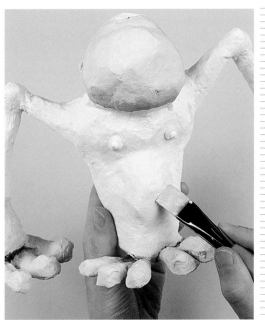

6 Paint the gorilla with a plaster of Paris mix (see page 8), leave to dry, then sand. Seal the gorilla with a coat of white emulsion paint and leave to dry. Paint the face, ears, hands, feet and chest flesh pink.

7 Paint the gorilla's fur grey. Shade the eye sockets in mid-brown. Using a fine paintbrush, add the nostrils and a mouth in dark brown.

8 Superglue two black beads in place for the eyes.

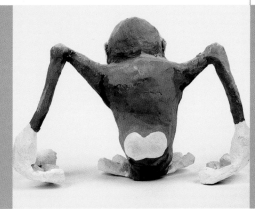

ORIENTAL DRAGON

SKILL LEVEL
★★

MATERIALS

template (page 118)
white paper
tracing paper
cardboard
newspaper
masking tape
PVA glue
strong wire for hanger
plaster of Paris
white emulsion paint
sandpaper
acrylic paints: pink, light green, dark green,
   orange, red, white, black
polymer clay
superglue
assorted beads
fine wire for necklace

TOOLS

black marker pen
scissors
paintbrushes
wire cutters
pencil

FINISHED SIZE:

H20cm x W24cm (H8 in. x W9½ in.)

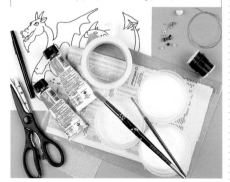

The design for this oriental dragon was inspired by Eastern textiles and embroidery. There is even a hint of the huge lizard dragons that are found on ancient Chinese blue-and-white china. His fire-breathing friend on page 67 is definitely a medieval dragon. Both are wearing decorative necklaces made by threading an assortment of beads and trinkets onto coloured wire.

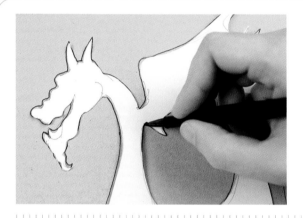

1 Trace the template on page 118 onto cardboard and cut it out.

2 Pad one side of the dragon shape with scrunched-up newspaper secured with masking tape.

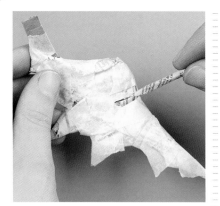

3 Cut out a second wing from cardboard and lightly pad it on one side. Make a thicker ridge running along the top of the wing and thin spines running down the wing by using thin rolls of newspaper hold in place with masking tape.

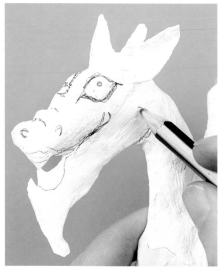

5 Paint the entire dragon with a plaster of Paris mix (see page 8), leave to dry, then sand. Seal with a coat of white emulsion paint and leave to dry. Draw in the facial details and body markings with a pencil.

4 Cover the dragon and the second wing with strips of newspaper dipped in PVA glue. Cut a small slit in the shoulder and insert the end of the separate wing. Secure the wing to the body with more strips of glued newspaper. Make a wire hanger and attach it to the back of the dragon with more glued strips.

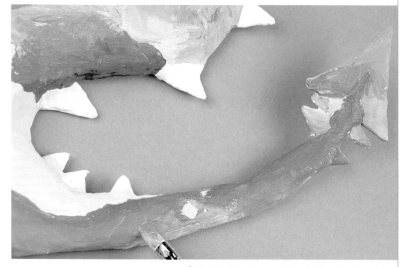

6 Paint the dragon's body in pink and green, adding spots in a bright, contrasting colour. Make the end of the tail red.

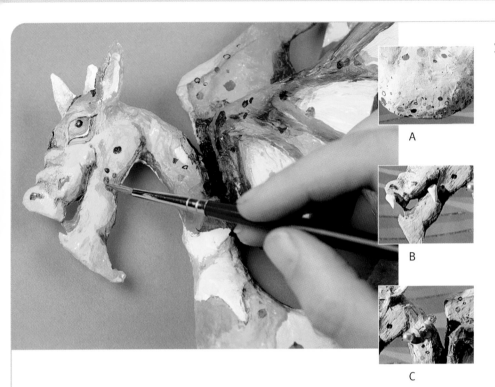

A

B

C

7 Shade the body in a darker shade of green at the base of the wings and along the edges of the dragon, particularly in the curves of the belly (A). Shade the bottom edge of the head in the same colour and paint in the facial details. Add orange eyes and a red tongue. Make tiny teeth from polymer clay and bake, following the manufacturer's instructions. When cool, and stick them in place with superglue (B). Thread coloured beads onto fine wire to make an exotic necklace to decorate the dragon's neck (C).

FLYING DRAGON

The main template for this handsome fellow (page 119) includes an arm and a leg. One more of each is made and added separately, along with two wings.

1 The curve of this dragon's wings help to create the impression that it is flying.

2 The dragon's hands are a version of the Glam Gecko's, on page 27.

MATERIALS
template (page 119)
see page 64 acrylic
paints:
  orange, green,
  red, blue, black,
  white

TOOLS
see page 64

FINISHED SIZE:
H43 cm x W41cm
(H17 in. x W16 in.)

JUGGLING IMPS

MATERIALS

white paper
tracing paper
cardboard
strong wire
newspaper
masking tape
PVA glue
plaster of Paris
white emulsion paint
sandpaper
acrylic paints: white,
   bright blue, light
   green, orange, gold,
   yellow, dark green,
   purple
decorative papers

superglue
large-headed pins
assorted bead and
   sequins
flat-backed gemstones

TOOLS

wire cutters
scissors
pencil
fine-tipped black marker
   pen
paintbrushes

FINISHED SIZE:

H30cm x W21.5cm
(H12 in. x W8½ in.)

Making imps is an opportunity to play with as many different colours and patterns as you wish. The bodies are built up on a simple base, but made more 3-D by curving up the cardboard. They can then be given personality by the skilful use of paint and decoupage. Give them long stripy socks and funny-shaped pointed hats, and use wrapping paper or small pieces of fabric to create clothes. The jolly Santa on page 72 shows how the idea can be adapted to create a seasonal character.

HAVE FUN DESIGNING YOUR OWN TEMPLATES FOR FANTASY FIGURES

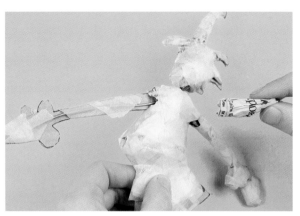

CREATE A HEAVENLY HOST OF ANGELS USING THIS TEMPLATE.

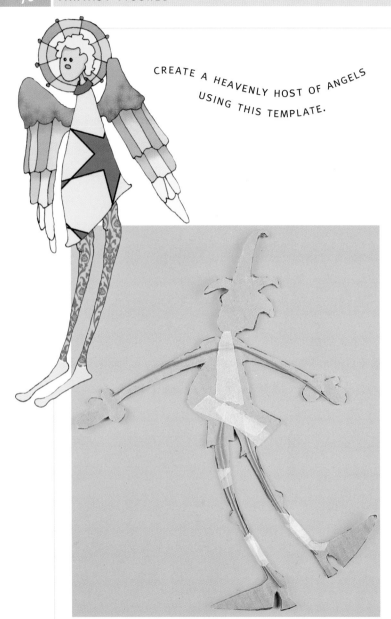

2 Pad one side of the body and head with scrunched-up newspaper held in place with masking tape. Tape in place rolls of newspaper to build up the limbs.

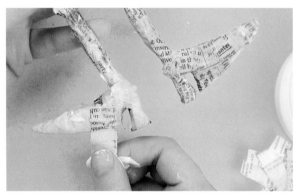

1 Trace the imp template on page 68 onto cardboard and cut out. Strengthen the arms and legs by taping a length of strong wire along the centre of each limb.

3 Cover the imp with strips of newspaper dipped in PVA glue. Make a wire hanger and fix it to the back of the imp with more glued strips. Leave to dry. Paint the imp with a plaster of Paris mix (see page 8), leave to dry, then sand. Seal the imp with a coat of white emulsion paint and leave to dry.

4 Paint on stripy stockings, a green shirt and orange and gold shoes.

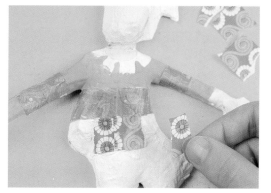

5 Using PVA glue, paste small pieces of patterned paper over the imp's body to make an attractive collage.

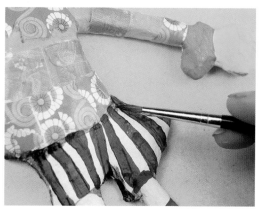

6 Paint the imp's yellow mittens and dark green stripy bloomers.

7 Decorate the imp's a multi-coloured hat. Paint the imp's face and give him a big moustache. Using superglue, stick decorative beads onto the body and hat.

TURN TO PAGE 72 FOR SANTA INSTRUCTIONS

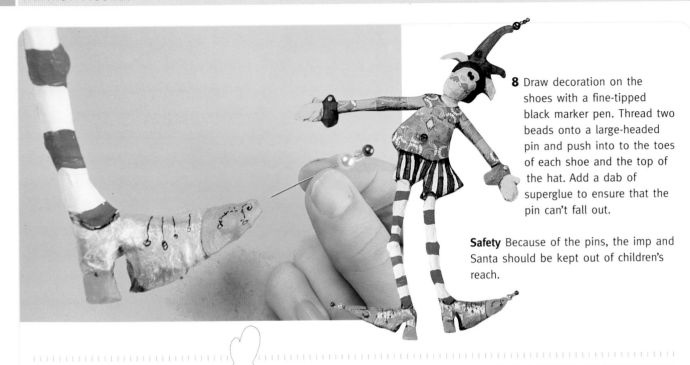

8 Draw decoration on the shoes with a fine-tipped black marker pen. Thread two beads onto a large-headed pin and push into to the toes of each shoe and the top of the hat. Add a dab of superglue to ensure that the pin can't fall out.

Safety Because of the pins, the imp and Santa should be kept out of children's reach.

MATERIALS
see page 68
thin wire for the spectacles

TOOLS
see page 68

FINISHED SIZE:
H30cm x W18cm
(H12 in. x W7 in.)

LEAPING SANTA

This leaping Santa sports a pair of spectacles and wonderful curled shoes. The nose is created by adding a ridge of cardboard to the face shape with strips of glued newspaper. As with the imps, a wire hanger attached to the back of the Santa allows him to be displayed on a wall.

1 Make spectacles for your santa by curving thin wire around the end of a skewer to make two loops,

2 Decorate the body with flat-backed gemstones in festive colours.

ROBOT

Science fiction films and Pop Art of the 1960s provided the inspiration for this robot whose body, head and feet are constructed from a series of boxes. Templates are provided, but you can construct a robot from any box shapes, although you may find it helpful to draw the design on graph paper first, to ensure you've got the proportions right.

I gave the robot extra-large feet, like many of my standing sculptures, for balance and stability. The hands and Frankenstein-like nuts and bolts all came from a local hardware store.

MATERIALS

templates (pages 120–121)
cardboard
newspaper
masking tape
PVA glue
plaster of Paris
white emulsion paint

sandpaper
acrylic paints: silver, light blue, dark
   blue, red, yellow, white, black
decorative papers
gemstones and small beads
superglue
nuts and bolts
crocodile clips
strong wire

TOOLS

pencil
ruler
scissors
paintbrushes
craft knife
wire cutters

FINISHED SIZE:

H28cm x W6cm x D4cm
(H11 in. x W2¼ in. x D1½ in.)

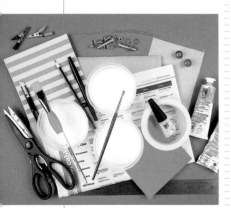

1 Use the templates provided or draw the robot's head, body and limb shapes on cardboard and cut out. (Remember that the robot is built up of box-like shapes, so each element – head, body and limbs – needs to have four sides.)

2 Assemble the body to form a box shape, with the shoulder protruding at the top, and secure with masking tape.

3 Tape a piece of cardboard over the base of the body, so that only the top end is open.

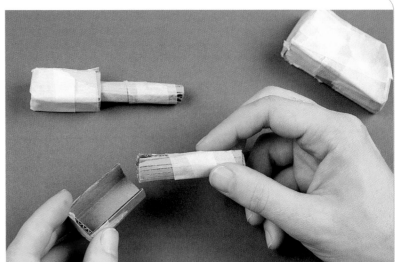

4 Using a craft knife, score parallel lines approximately 5mm (¼ in.) apart along a strip of cardboard, taking care not to cut all the way through. With the cuts on the outside, bend the strip around to form a curved piece.

6 Make two large feet in the same way as you made the head in Steps 4 and 5. Make two small boxes for the robot's shoulders and form the arms from rolls of scored cardboard. Tape a third of the arm into the box.

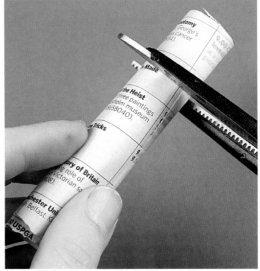

5 Cut a strip of cardboard with curves each end for the head. Score then bend the strip into three sections, as shown, then tape the scored strip from Step 4 over the open end to complete the head.

7 Make rolls of newspaper secured with masking tape for the legs and robot neck. Attach the legs to the feet and the neck to the head with masking tape.

10 Paint the main body silver, the control panel and feet light blue, and the head dark blue with white and red details.

8 Make a small box for the control panel and tape it to the centre front of the body. Cover all the body pieces with strips of newspaper dipped in PVA glue. Join them together with more strips of glued paper.

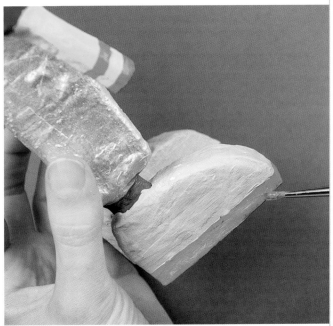

9 Using a craft knife, make a hole in the top of the body and fix the neck in place with PVA glue. When the robot had dried, paint it with a plaster of Paris mix (see page 8), leave to dry, then sand. Seal with a coat of white emulsion paint.

11 Paint the shoulders blue and the arms red and yellow, and paint a red stripe on the feet.

12 Cut a piece of blue-and-yellow striped paper slightly narrower than the width of the body and stick it just below the control panel. Then cut a frame of red paper to go over the striped paper, leaving more paper on the right-hand side so that there's room for the 'control buttons'.

13 Stick three tiny blue gemstones down the right-hand edge of the red frame, a strip of yellow paper down the left-hand edge of the control panel and a tiny square of red paper in the bottom right corner. Add a tiny yellow bead to the left of the square, and a small glass bead to the centre.

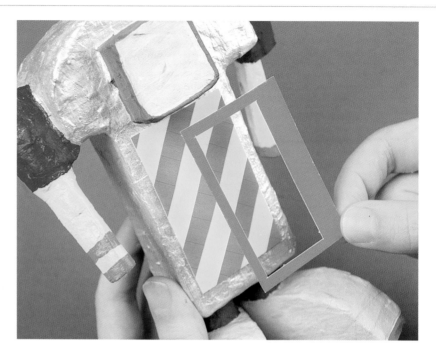

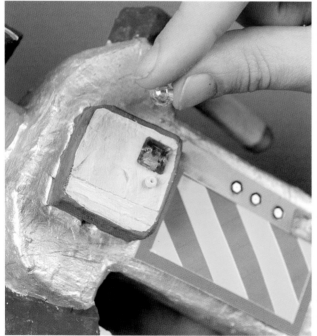

14 Using a craft knife, cut two small holes in the head for the eyes. Push two large red beads into the holes so that they sit partially below the surface and superglue them in place.

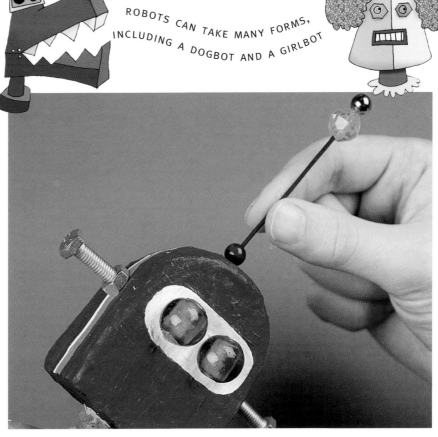

ROBOTS CAN TAKE MANY FORMS, INCLUDING A DOGBOT AND A GIRLBOT

15 Using a craft knife, cut two holes in the side of the robot's head, insert two nuts and bolts, and superglue them in place.

16 Using a craft knife, make a small hole in the top of the head and superglue a length of strong wire decorated with shiny beads into the hole to form the antenna.

ROBOT ANGLES

THE LOOK OF YOUR ROBOT WILL DEPEND VERY MUCH ON THE BITS AND PIECES YOU USE FOR DECORATION. I USED WASHERS AROUND THE EDGES OF THE FEET AND GLUED CROCODILE CLIPS TO THE ENDS OF THE ARMS FOR HANDS.

MONSTERS, INC.

MATERIALS

spectacles template
  (page 122)
white paper
cardboard
newspaper
masking tape
PVA glue
plaster of Paris
white emulsion paint
sandpaper
acrylic paints: orange,
  green, blue, pink, dark
  blue, purple, yellow,
  brown, black, white, gold
- superglue
- pink glitter nail polish
- polymer clay

TOOLS

- pencil
- ruler
- scissors
- paintbrushes
- craft knife

FINISHED SIZE:

H25cm x W13cm x D10cm
(H10 in. x W5 in. x D4 in.)

BODY PARTS
you will need...

Body Legs Feet Horns Hair

Like the Robot on page 74, these space monsters are inspired by the art and films of the 1960s. Gordon from the Gamma Zone (*far right*) is painted in a flat, multi-coloured Pop Art style. I've given him huge feet to help with gravity and decorated his immense toe nails with glitter nail polish. Doris from Delta 4, his partner (*right*), has a large gingham bow on her head and pointed blue sparkly specs. She is the perfect 'Space Housewife'!

1 Sketch out a monster to use as a guide or follow the body parts panel, left.

2 Trace the body shape onto cardboard and cut it out. Pad both sides with scrunched-up newspaper secured with masking tape.

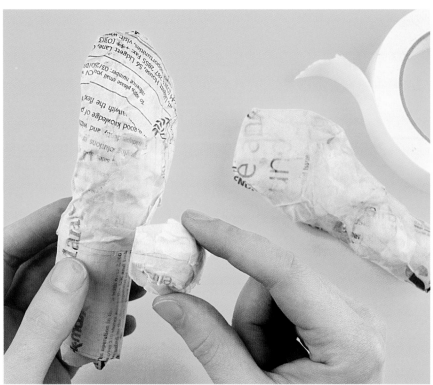

4 Make legs by scrunching up newspaper and wrapping masking tape around them. Make two balls from scrunched-up newspaper and tape them to the legs to make knobbly knees.

3 Pad the front of the body with extra newspaper to give the monster a round tummy.

5 Cut out two large feet from cardboard and pad one side with scrunched-up newspaper attached with masking tape.

6 Cover the monster's body and legs with strips of newspaper dipped in PVA glue. Tape the legs to the body and cover the joins with more glued newspaper.

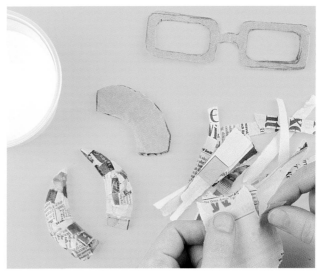

8 Cut horns, a pair of glasses (template on page 122) and a Mohican hair style from cardboard. Pad the horns and Mohican crest with newspaper and masking tape. Cover all the pieces with strips of newspaper dipped in PVA glue.

7 Fix the feet to the legs with plenty of masking tape and cover the joins with more glued strips.

9 Using PVA glue, attach the Mohican hair to the monster's head. Cut two holes in the sides of the head with a craft knife. Insert the horns and fix in place with PVA glue.

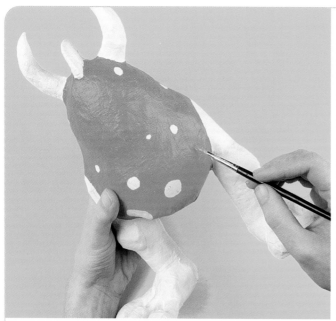

10 When the glue has dried, paint the monster with a plaster of Paris mix (see page 8), leave to dry, then sand. Seal with a coat of white emulsion paint and leave to dry. Paint the body orange, leaving a few white areas.

11 Paint the white spots green, give the legs blue, gold and pink stripes, and paint the feet dark blue. When the paint has dried, coat the toe nails with pink glitter nail polish.

12 Paint the horns purple and the Mohican hair yellow and brown. Paint the glasses black with a green outline. When dry, glue them to the monster's head.

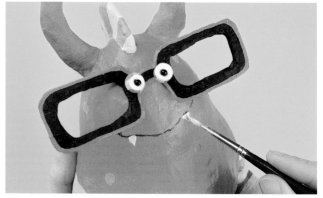

13 Make two discs for eyes from polymer clay and bake, following the manufacturer's instructions. Paint the eyes white and glue them in place across the bridge of the spectacles. Glue on black beads for the pupils. Paint a fine black line for the mouth and add two white teeth, one at each corner.

MONSTER ANGLES

YOU CAN LET YOUR IMAGINATION RUN WILD WHEN DESIGNING FANTASY FIGURES LIKE THIS MONSTER. PART OF THE CHARM IS IN THE USE OF BLOCKS OF BOLD POP-ART STYLE COLOUR. THE LARGE FEET AND KNOBBLY KNEES HELP TO KEEP THE MONSTER UPRIGHT AND THE SPECTACLES ADD TO ITS APPEAL.

DORIS FROM DELTA 4

Both monsters sport spectacles, but Doris's are of a rather glitzy design. Cut out cardboard frames and cover them with a layer of glitter.

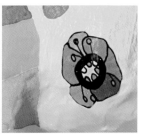

1 Make discs for eyes out of polymer clay and add a separate eyelid. Bake, and when cool, glue the black beads on top.

2 Decorate the monster with flowers cut from sheets of wrapping paper.

MATERIALS
see page 80
acrylic paint:
  yellow, green,
  orange, red,
  pink, blue
glitter
wrapping paper
length of gingham
  ribbon

TOOLS
see page 80

FINISHED SIZE:
H25cm x W13cm x D10cm
(H10 in. x W5 in. x D4 in.)

SKILL LEVEL ★★ COW CLOCK

When making this clock, there are some practical issues to consider. The sides of the moon need to be deep enough to contain the clock mechanism. (These are sold by most good craft shops.) The dimensions of the moon's face itself will depend on the length of the clock hands. Before painting on the moon face design, remember to measure and mark the position of the clock mechanism so that the two design elements do not overlap.

MATERIALS

dinner plate to draw around
strong cardboard
newspaper
masking tape
PVA adhesive
template (page 122)
tracing paper
white paper
strong wire for hanger
superglue
stick or short length of
  gardening cane
plaster of Paris
white emulsion paint
sandpaper
handmade textured paper

acrylic paints: pale blue,
  black, white, pink, brown,
  dark blue, silver, green
clock mechanism

TOOLS

pencil
scissors
ruler
wire cutters
paintbrushes
craft knife

FINISHED SIZE:

Clock diameter 25.5cm (10 in.)
Cow H6–8cm (2½–3 in.)

1 Draw around a dinner plate on cardboard and cut out. Cut a long strip of cardboard (you may have to join two pieces together) wider than the thickness of the clock mechanism. Score down it at 5mm (¼ in.) intervals, taking care not to cut all the way through.

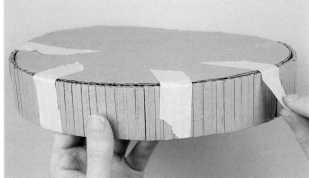

2 Bend the strip around the edge of the cardboard circle, scored side out. Cut to length and tape in place.

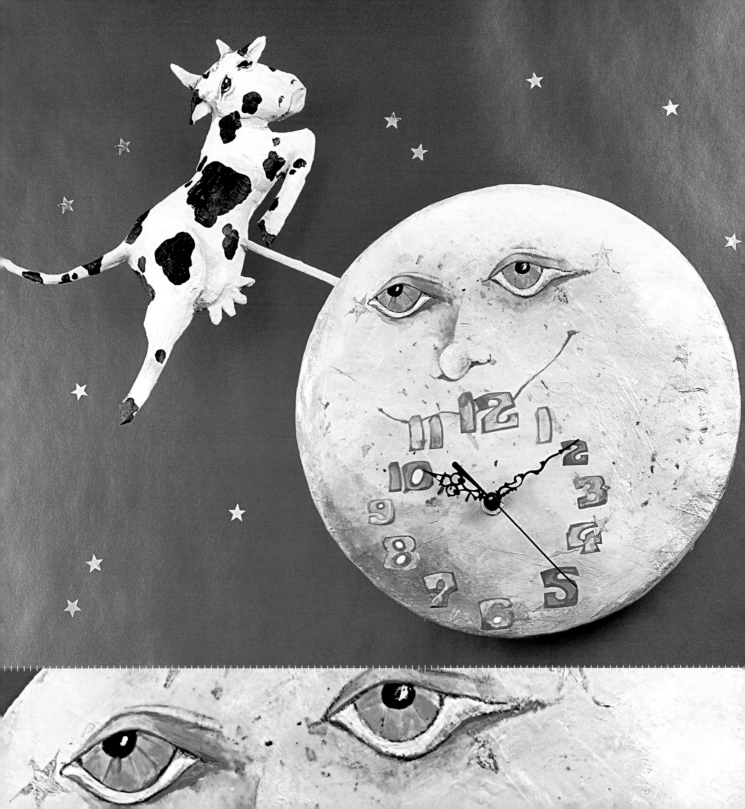

3 Begin to pad out the front and sides of the clock with scrunched-up newspaper secured with masking tape. Add extra padding where the moon's face will be.

5 Trace the cow template on page 122 onto cardboard and cut out. Alternatively, draw your chosen animal shape.

6 Pad the front of the cow with scrunched-up newspaper secured with masking tape. Cover it with strips of newspaper dipped in PVA glue.

4 When complete, cover the front and sides with strips of newspaper dipped in PVA glue. Cut half a circle of cardboard and attach it to the back of the clock with masking tape at the top of what will be the clock face. Cover the back with more glued strips of newspaper.

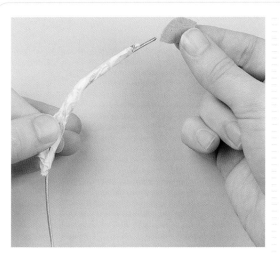

7 Cut a piece of strong wire for the tail. Wrap a strip of newspaper around the wire and secure it with masking tape. Cut a leaf shape from card and fix it to one end of the tail with PVA glue. Wrap strips of newspaper dipped in PVA around the wire, leaving a short piece uncovered.

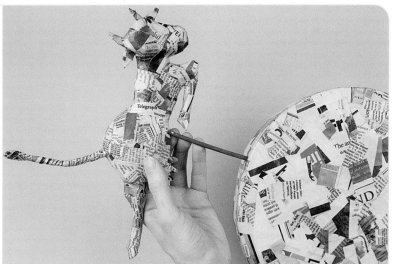

9 Push one end of a stick or short gardening cane into the cow's belly and secure it with PVA glue. Push the other end into the clock at an angle of what will be 10 or 11 o'clock to make it look as though the cow is 'jumping over the moon'. Secure the stick on the back with strips of newspaper dipped in PVA glue and leave to dry.

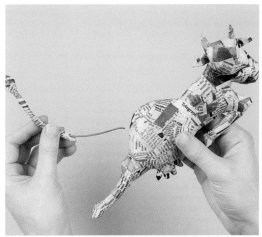

8 Using a pin, make a small hole in the rear of the cow. Insert the unwrapped wire of the tail piece, and secure it with a dab of PVA glue.

10 Paint both the clock and the cow with a plaster of Paris mix (see page 8), leave to dry, then sand. Seal both pieces with a coat of white emulsion paint and leave to dry. Paint a base colour of pale blue over the moon's face.

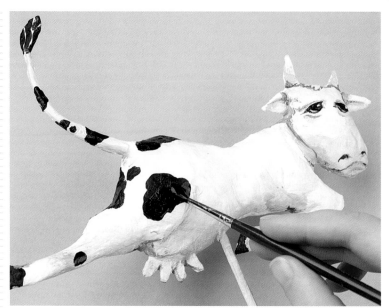

11 Using PVA, which will dry clear, glue pieces of torn, handmade paper over the moon's face to give it an interesting texture.

12 Paint the cow with black and white markings, then add a pink nose, ears and udders and large brown eyes.

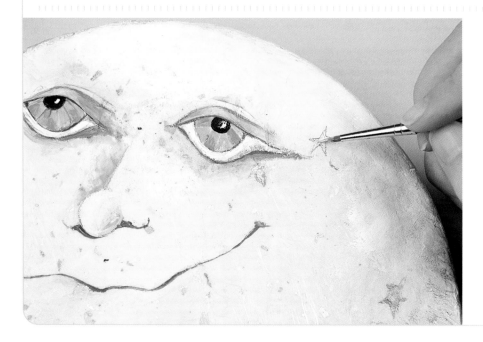

13 Measure and lightly mark the position of the clock mechanism near the bottom of the clock. Using blues, greens and silvers (follow the photo for guidance), paint a face towards the top left of the moon, giving it a wide, sleepy smile. Paint the eyes with large, dreamy eyelids.

14 Lightly mark the position of the numbers on the clock face. Trace the numbers on the template onto blue paper, cut them out and stick them in position. Alternatively, paint the numbers directly onto the clock face.

17 Attach the clock hands.

15 Using a craft knife, make a hole in the centre of the numbers large enough for the clock spindle.

16 Insert the clock mechanism.

ELEPHANT MIRROR FRAME

SKILL LEVEL
★ ★ ★

MATERIALS

template (page 123)
strong cardboard
newspaper
masking tape
PVA glue
plaster of Paris
white emulsion paint
sandpaper
acrylic paints: pale blue,
   dark blue, white, red,
   pink, yellow
strong wire for hanger
mirror tile
superglue
decorative papers

gemstones and beads,
   including a large one
   for the eye
large-headed pin

TOOLS

black marker pen
ruler
scissors
wire cutters
paintbrushes
craft knife

FINISHED SIZE:

H61cm x W41cm
(H24 in. x W16 in.)

The elephant mirror frame is made around a bathroom mirror tile, although you could use any piece of mirror. You need at least 2 cm (¾ in.) of cardboard around the mirror to make a secure frame. Like many of the designs in this book, this piece is highly decorated. There is a collage of coloured, patterned papers on the elephant's turban and stomach. Extra sparkle has also been added. If you intend to place it in a bathroom, paint the frame with several layers of varnish when finished to protect it from the damp environment.

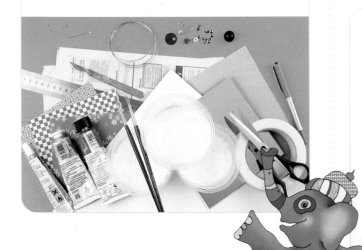

WHY NOT TRY MAKING A CLOCK INSTEAD OF A MIRROR (SEE PAGES 86–91)?

1 Trace the elephant template onto cardboard and cut out. Make sure the frame will be large enough to accommodate the mirror tile.

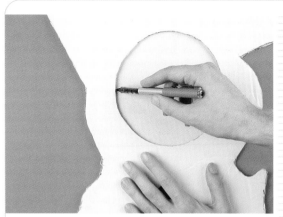

2 Draw around the elephant shape onto another sheet of cardboard and cut out a second elephant. Mark a circle in the centre of one elephant that is at least 2cm (¾ in.) smaller than the mirror and cut it out. Place the elephant with the hole on top of the solid elephant. Draw around the inside of the circle onto the lower elephant.

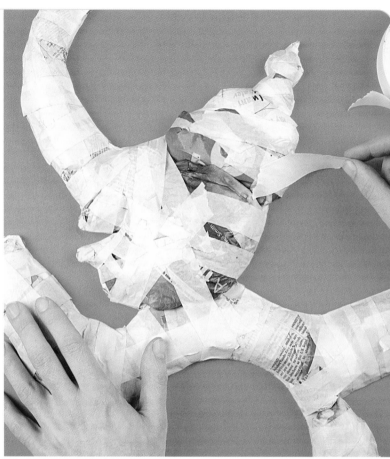

3 Place the elephant with the hole to one side. Place the mirror tile over the marked circle on the other piece of cardboard and draw around it. Cut out the square shape. Stick the elephant with the round hole on top of the elephant with the square hole with PVA glue.

4 Pad the front of the elephant shape with scrunched-up newspaper and secure with masking tape.

5 Make a large, oval ear following the method given on pages 30 to 32. Cut out small semi-circle for an eyelid from the same layered newspaper.

6 Push the sides of the ear together to form wrinkles and attach the ear to the elephant's head with strips of newspaper dipped in PVA glue.

7 Fix the eyelid to the elephant's head with strips of newspaper dipped in PVA glue. Leave the frame to dry overnight.

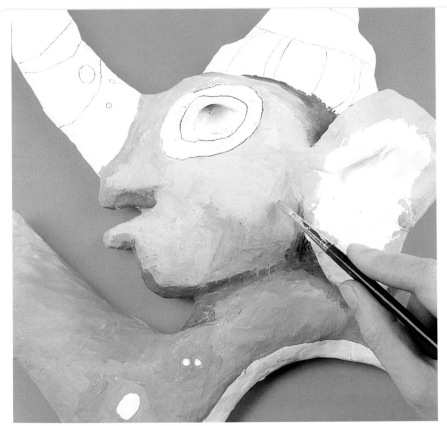

9 Make a wire loop hanger and attach it to the back of the elephant with plenty of strips of newspaper dipped in PVA glue. Leave to dry.

8 Paint the frame with a plaster of Paris mix (see page 8), leave to dry, then sand. Seal the frame with a coat of white emulsion paint and leave to dry. Draw in the elephant's markings in pencil. Paint the elephant pale blue, with darker blue shadows under the chin and turban and around the legs.

10 Paint the back of the mirror white to give it a nice finish. Paint the inner rim, where the mirror will sit, red. Superglue the mirror in place at the back of the frame.

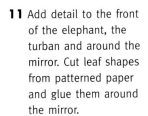

11 Add detail to the front of the elephant, the turban and around the mirror. Cut leaf shapes from patterned paper and glue them around the mirror.

12 For extra sparkle around the mirror, glue gemstones to the tips of alternate leaves.

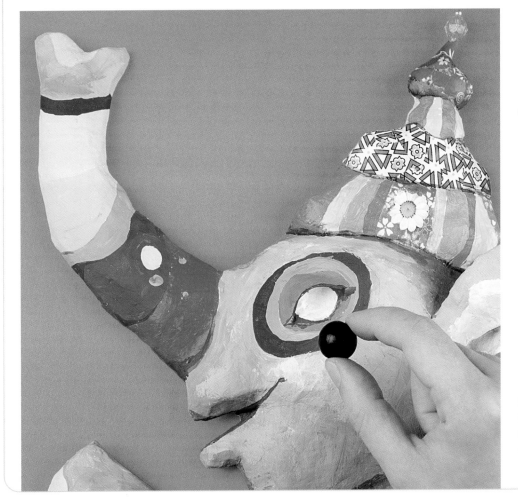

13 Paint coloured stripes on the turban and add decorative papers. Thread beads onto a large-headed pin, then push the pin into the top of the turban and secure it with a dab of superglue. Using PVA, glue a cut-out paper flower to the centre of the turban. Finally, glue a big, black bead into the elephant's eye socket, beneath the eyelid.

Safety Because of the pin in the turban, the elephant should be kept out of children's reach.

VINTAGE CAR

The vintage car (*far right*) has tiny wheels to emphasise the square shape of the body. In contrast, the orange bubble car (*right*) has a rounded shape and big, bouncy wheels. I decorated the old green car with stamps in a matching colour, but you could cover it with mosaic pieces cut from a magazine or newspapers. Kitchen foil can be used for the headlights and the car can be given its own personalised number plate.

MATERIALS

templates (pages 124–125)
tracing paper
white paper
cardboard
masking tape
newspaper
PVA glue
plaster of Paris
white emulsion paint
sandpaper
acrylic paints: dark green, light
 green, red, silver, black, white
superglue

stamps or decorative paper
assorted flat-backed gemstones

TOOLS

black marker pen
scissors
craft knife
ruler
paintbrushes

FINISHED SIZE:

H19cm x W3cm x D18cm
(H7½ in. x W2 in. x D7 in.)

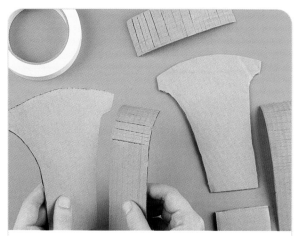

1 Trace the templates on pages 124–125 onto cardboard and cut out. Using a craft knife and ruler, score parallel lines about 5mm (¼ in.) apart on the strips for the front, back and roof of the car, taking care not to cut all the way through the cardboard.

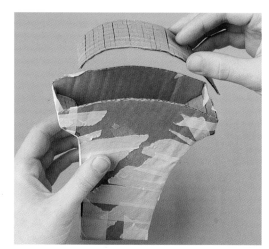

2 Join the pieces of the car body together with masking tape to form a box shape.

3 Make two more boxes for the boot and the bonnet. Score lines in the tops of the boxes so that the cardboard can be bent to create a curved top.

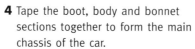

4 Tape the boot, body and bonnet sections together to form the main chassis of the car.

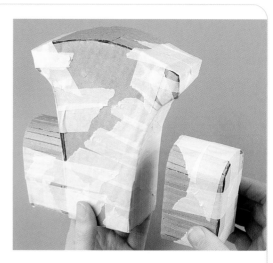

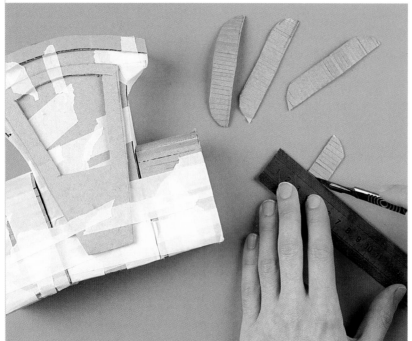

5 Cut out four mudguards, two car door shapes and two strips for the sides of the roof.

6 Cover the mudguards, door shapes and roof pieces in newspaper strips dipped in PVA glue. Using PVA, glue all these pieces in place.

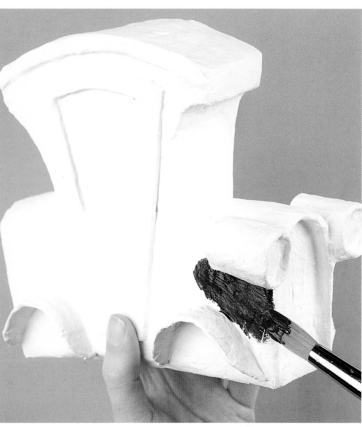

7 Make four wheels from discs of card with a ring of card glued on the front. Cover with strips of newspaper dipped in PVA glue.

8 Cut out two strips of cardboard and slightly score them so they will bend. Using tape, wrap each one around a small disc to form a cylinder.

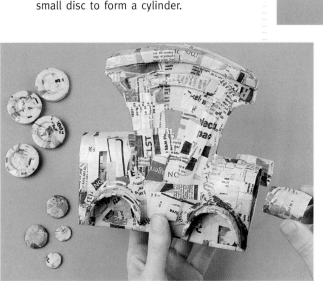

9 Cut out two more small and two very small discs from cardboard; these will be the supports for the brake lights and indicators. Cover all these pieces with newspaper strips dipped in PVA glue. Attach the headlights to the front of the car with more glued newspaper strips.

10 Paint the car with a plaster of Paris mix (see page 8), leave to dry, then sand. Seal the car with a coat of white emulsion paint and leave to dry. Paint the whole car dark green.

11 Highlight details in light green, paint the door red and add a red stripe to the mudguards. Cut out two door frames and a rectangle for the roof from thin paper and decorate with old stamps or decorative paper. Stick them to the car with PVA glue.

12 Paint the headlights silver and stick on gems for the lights. Glue gems to the small discs and fix to the car.

CAR ANGLES

THE SHAPE OF THIS CAR BRINGS TO MIND VEHICLES FROM THE BEGINNING OF THE TWENTIETH CENTURY. THE PASSENGER AND COLOUR SCHEME WERE CHOSEN TO EMPHASISE ITS PERIOD CHARM.

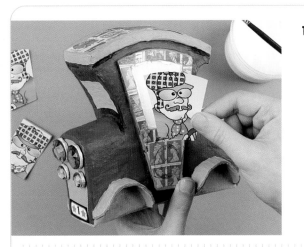

13 Photocopy the illustrations provided for the driver and front grill of the car. Alternatively, paint your own designs or cut out pictures from magazines. Stick them in place with PVA glue.

14 Paint the wheels black and silver. Photocopy the illustrations provided for the spokes (or paint your own) and stick them in place. Attach the wheels securely to the chassis with PVA glue.

BUBBLE CAR

We've included the bubble car to demonstrate the different effect that can be achieved by using another painting style.

1 The car is painted in a bold style reminiscent of the 1970s.

2 Decoupage flowers enhance the hippy feel.

BOOK ENDS

The inspiration for the pattern on these book ends came from tiles that I saw on a trip to Andalucia in Southern Spain, which had a repeating geometric pattern in terracotta and azure blue. You can use the tile patterns provided or draw your own and copy them on a computer or photocopier. Alternatively, you could cut tiles from wrapping paper or paint the book ends with multi-coloured shapes. The instructions are to make a single book end, so follow them twice to make two.

MATERIALS
templates (pages 126–127)
strong cardboard
newspaper
masking tape
PVA glue
plaster of Paris
white emulsion paint
sandpaper
acrylic paints: cream, brown,
  light blue, dark blue, black,
  white, yellow ochre
piping cord
decorative paper

TOOLS
black marker pen
pencil
ruler
scissors
paintbrushes
craft knife

FINISHED SIZE:
Book End H20cm x W24cm x
D14cm (H8 in. x W9½ in. x
D5½ in.)
Finial H12cm x W6cm (H4¾ in. x
W2½ in.)

1 Using the templates provided, cut out all the pieces needed to make a book end from strong cardboard. Start to assemble the book end by taping one of the stepped sides to the back piece.

2 Attach the second side and the bottom piece with more tape.

4 Tape on the top of the book end.

3 Tape in place the front upright and stepped sections.

5 Place the book end onto the base piece and attach with tape.

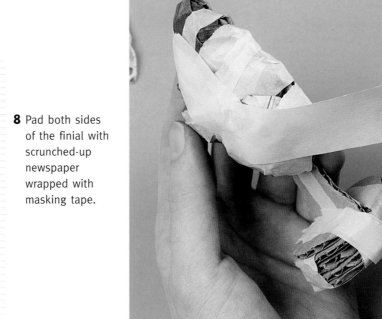

8 Pad both sides of the finial with scrunched-up newspaper wrapped with masking tape.

6 Trace the pineapple finial, two half-circles and four base circles onto cardboard and cut out. Tape the two base circles together.

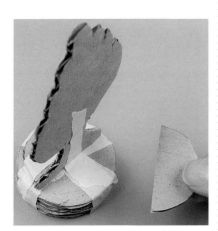

9 Cover the book end and the finial with strips of newspaper dipped in PVA glue. Stick a length of piping cord around the base of the finial with more PVA glue and leave to dry.

7 Tape the finial to the base and place a half circle either side to secure it in position. The half circles are slightly smaller than the base circles, creating a small ridge for the piping cord.

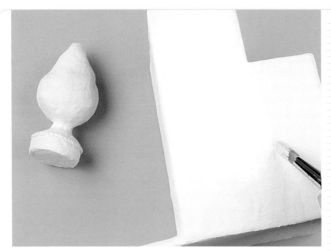

10 Paint both elements with a plaster of Paris mix (see page 8), leave to dry, then sand. Seal with a coat of white emulsion paint and leave to dry. Paint with a cream base coat.

12 Cut out the 'tiles' and glue them in position with PVA glue.

11 Draw and colour your own tile patterns or photocopy the design provided.

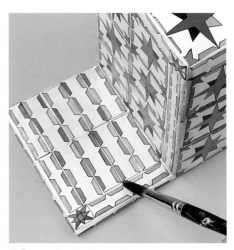

13 Age the book end by applying a coat of very dilute brown paint.

14 Paint the finial in a blue-and-white checkerboard design.

15 Glue the finial in position on the top of the book end.

BOOK ANGLES

THE WEIGHT OF THE BOOKS ON THE BOTTOM PANEL OF THE BOOK END HOLDS IT IN POSITION. FOR A SIMPLER DESIGN, GLUE A READY-MADE BOX ONTO A BASE PANEL, COVER WITH GLUED STRIPS AND DECORATE!

TOUCAN VASE

SKILL LEVEL
★★

The toucan vase is shaped around a plastic, waterproof beaker. It is given a more elegant form with the addition of a 10cm (4 in.) circular base made from a ring of cardboard. The birds' beaks and the leaves need to be placed carefully around the vase for balance. The vase can then be decorated in the vibrant colours of a tropical rainforest. Protect the vases with at least two coats of a non-toxic varnish.

The poppy vase (page 115) is made around an old plastic water bottle. Its petals are made separately and glued in place, with an exotic bead forming the flower centre.

MATERIALS
templates (page 127)
tracing paper
white paper
plastic beaker
cardboard
newspaper
masking tape
PVA glue
plaster of Paris
white emulsion paint

sandpaper
acrylic paints: red, light
    green, dark green,
    orange, yellow, white,
    black, purple, blue
superglue
4 black beads for eyes

TOOLS
black marker pen
pencil

ruler
scissors
paintbrushes
craft knife

FINISHED SIZE:
Diameter 9cm (3½ in.)
H19cm (7½ in.)

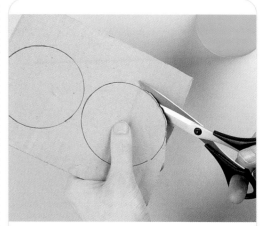

1 From cardboard, cut two circles the same diameter as the widest part of the waterproof beaker that you intend to use as the inner vase.

2 Cut a length of cardboard approximately 10cm (4 in.) taller than the waterproof container. Score parallel lines 5mm (¼ in.) apart along the length of the card, taking care not to cut all the way through.

5 Set aside the stand, and fix the roll of cardboard cut in Step 3 around a disc with masking tape to make the outer vase.

3 Roll the card around one of the discs made in Step 1 and mark the exact length needed. Cut to size.

4 Before making up the vase, measure the distance between the bottom of the beaker and the end of the card. Cut a strip of cardboard to this depth and 10cm (4 in.) long. Score it as before, tape the ends together to form a circle and attach it with masking tape to the centre of the second cardboard disc made in Step 1. This will act as a stand for the waterproof container.

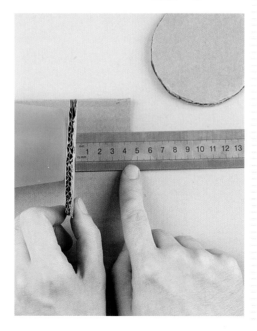

6 Apply PVA glue to the base of the stand made in Step 4 and insert it into the tube, pressing it down gently but firmly to ensure that it sticks to the base of the tube. This forms a false bottom to support the plastic container and make the vase taller and more elegant.

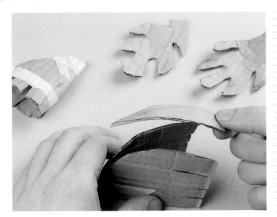

7 Using the templates on page 127, cut out two tropical leaf shapes and two birds' beaks from cardboard. The beaks are made more 3-D by adding a triangular gusset along the bottom.

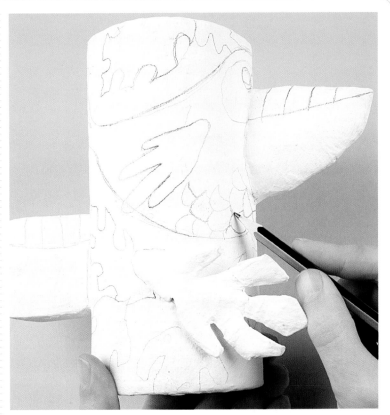

8 Cover the vase, beaks and leaves with strips of newspaper dipped in PVA glue. Fix the beaks opposite each other and at different heights for balance. Glue the leaves in the spaces in between. Leave to dry.

9 Paint with a plaster of Paris mix (see page 8), leave to dry, then sand. Seal the vase with a coat of white emulsion paint and leave to dry. Draw a tropical leaf and toucan design on the vase in pencil, using the illustrations on page 111 as a guide.

10 Paint the inside of the vase red. Add jungle leaves in greens and yellows around the outside.

11 Paint the birds' beaks in orange with yellow, blue and orange stripes. Paint their bodies in bright, cheerful colours.

12 Outline parts of the design with a fine black pen. Superglue on small black beads for the birds' eyes.

TOUCAN ANGLES

BIRD BOOKS ARE FULL OF INSPIRATION FOR TROPICAL BIRD DESIGNS. THE KEY THING WITH THESE VASES IS TO ENSURE THE BEAKS ARE PLACED WHERE THEY BALANCE EACH OTHER OUT. ADDING MORE LEAVES ALLOWS YOU TO ADJUST THE BALANCE, WHERE NECESSARY.

POPPY VASE

This vase was created by applying strips of newspaper dipped in PVA glue directly onto a plastic bottle. It was then sealed and decorated with brightly coloured flowers, each of which was created from individual petals that are drawn freehand.

MATERIALS
see page 110
acrylic paints:
    cream, light green,
    dark green, red,
    purple, orange,
    yellow, black

4 beads for
    stamens

TOOLS
see page 110

FINISHED SIZE:
Diameter 11cm (4½ in.)
H26cm (10¼ in.)

1 Paint each petal a different tone of red, purple or orange before joining them together with superglue. In the centre, glue a bead over a rubber washer to form a stamen.

2 Paint flower stems onto vase. Add a border of green grass to the bottom edge of the vase.

TEMPLATES

This chapter contains all the templates used in this book. The templates are shown actual size unless otherwise stated. Where necessary, enlarge the templates on a photocopier by the percentage given, and then trace around them.

NIGHT OWL

PAGE 14

Owl Base

Beak

Foot x 2

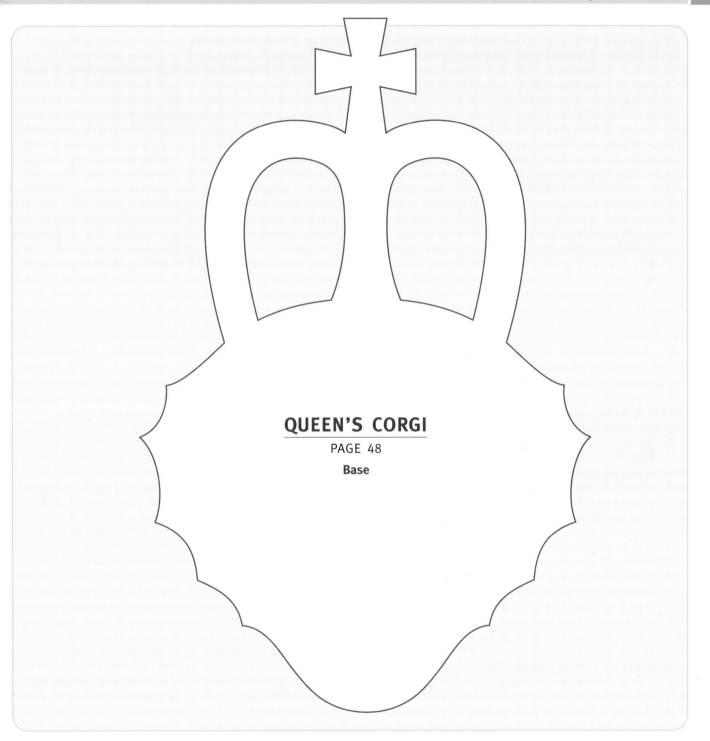

QUEEN'S CORGI
PAGE 48

Base

ORIENTAL DRAGON

PAGE 64

Enlarge by 20%

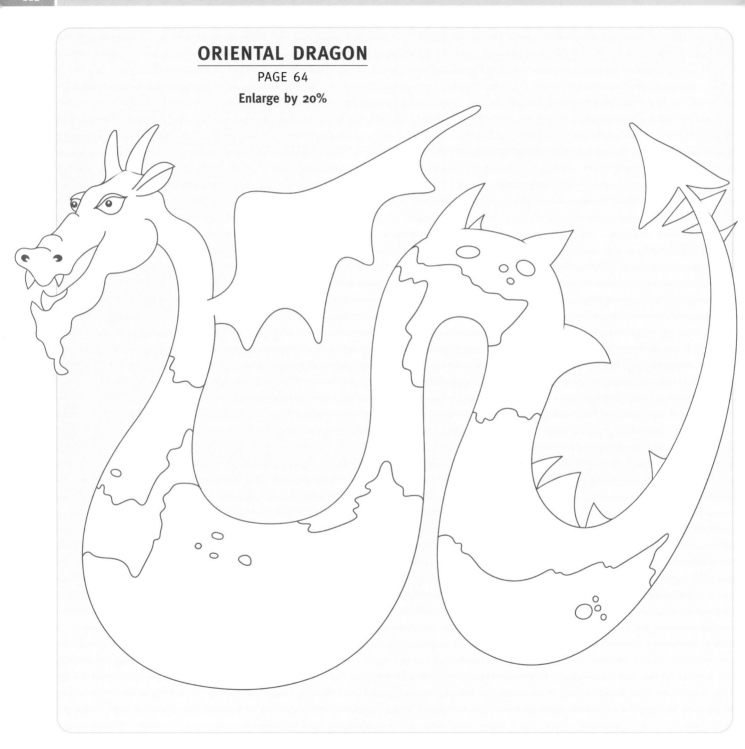

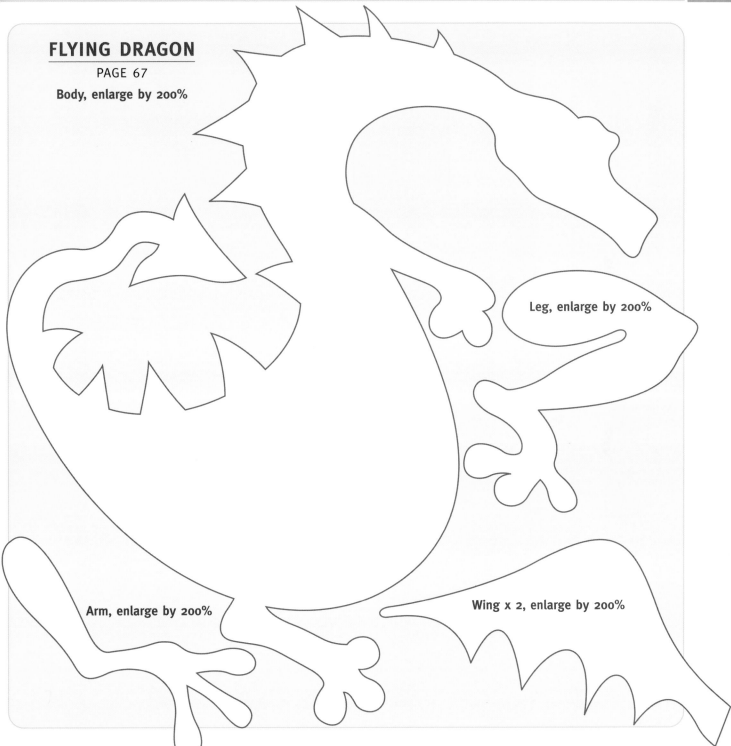

FLYING DRAGON

PAGE 67

Body, enlarge by 200%

Leg, enlarge by 200%

Arm, enlarge by 200%

Wing x 2, enlarge by 200%

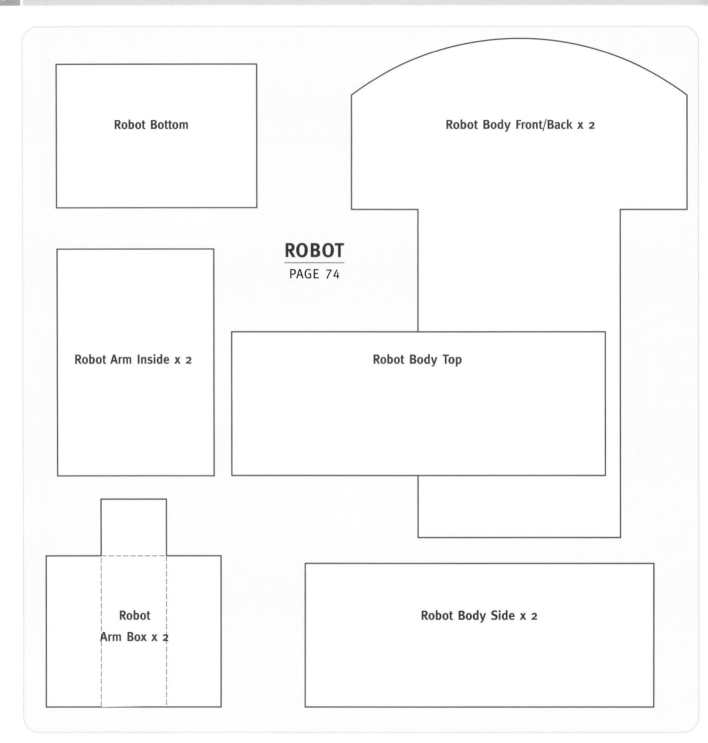

Robot Bottom

Robot Body Front/Back x 2

ROBOT
PAGE 74

Robot Arm Inside x 2

Robot Body Top

Robot
Arm Box x 2

Robot Body Side x 2

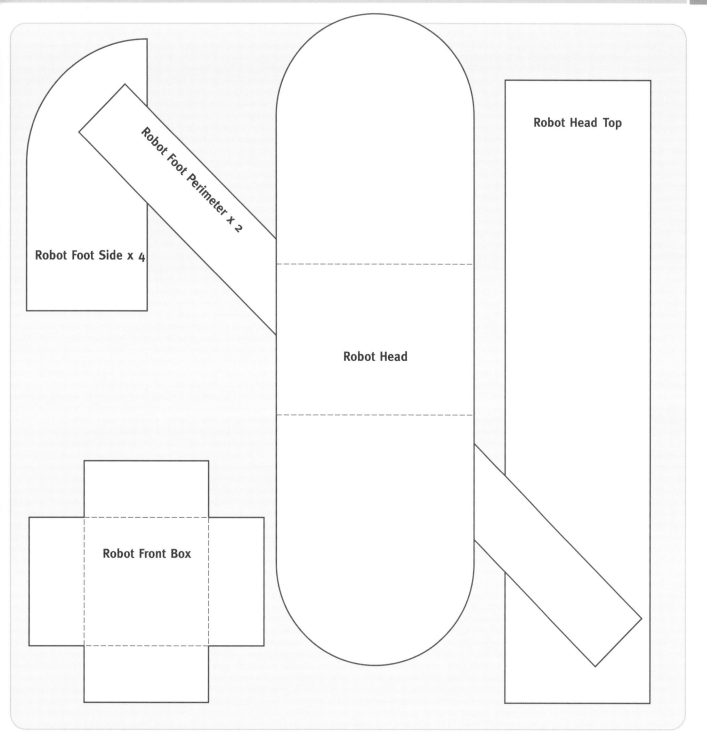

Robot Head Top

Robot Foot Perimeter x 2

Robot Foot Side x 4

Robot Head

Robot Front Box

MONSTERS, INC.
PAGE 80
Glasses

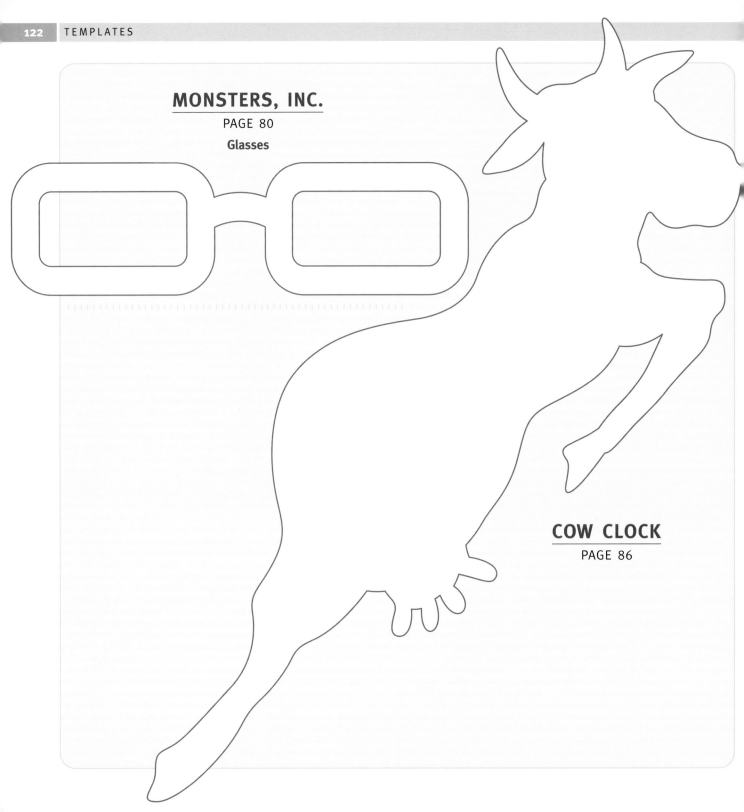

COW CLOCK
PAGE 86

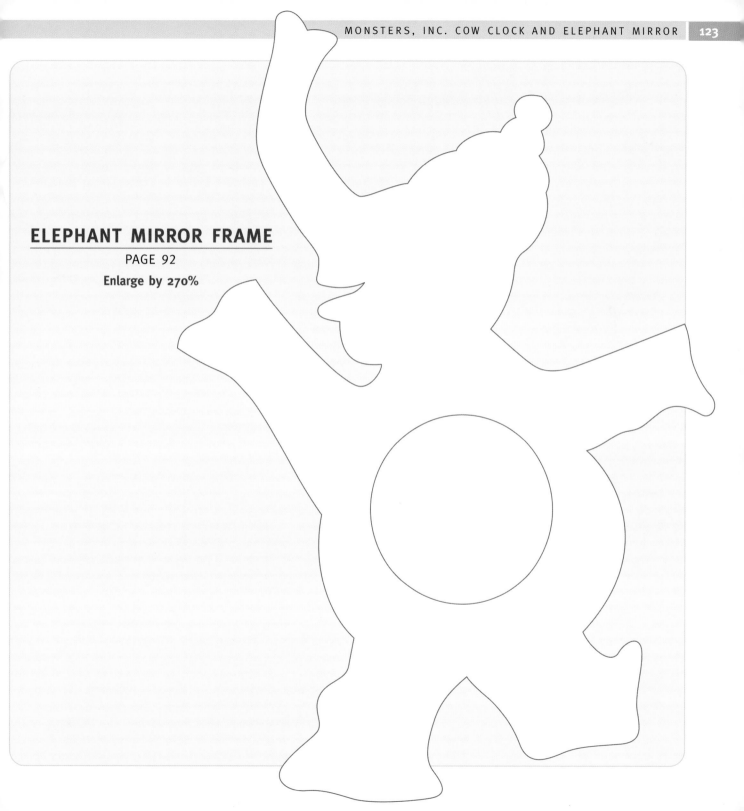

ELEPHANT MIRROR FRAME
PAGE 92
Enlarge by 270%

VINTAGE CAR
PAGE 98

Photocopy and use these
illustrations to decorate
your sculpture.
Enlarge by 200%

Side Windows x 2

Front

Fender

Wheel Hubs x 4

Car Bonnet Top

Car Wheel x 4

Car Door x 2

Car Headlights x 2

Car Wheel Ring x 4

Car Small
Discs x 2

Car Boot Top,
enlarge by 200%

Car Tiny
Discs x 2

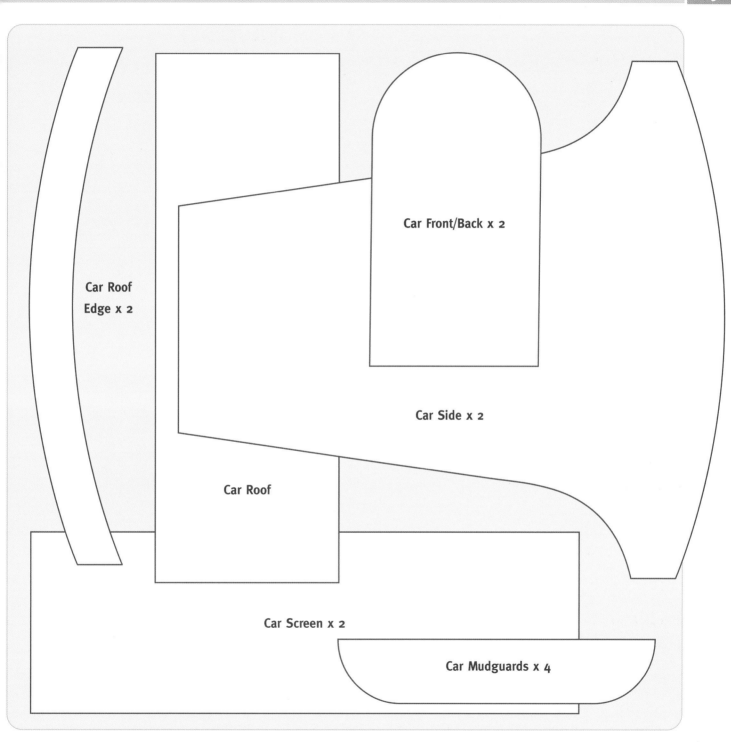

Car Roof
Edge x 2

Car Front/Back x 2

Car Side x 2

Car Roof

Car Screen x 2

Car Mudguards x 4

BOOK ENDS

PAGE 104

Book End Base, enlarge by 200%

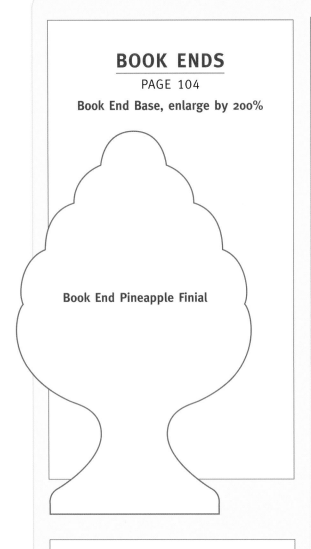

Book End Pineapple Finial

Book End Top for Step/Step Upright x 2, enlarge by 200%

Book End Back, enlarge by 133%

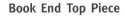

Front upright, enlarge by 133%

Pineapple Finial Base Half Circle x 2

Book End Top Piece

Photocopy and use these illustrations to decorate your sculpture.

Enlarge by 200%

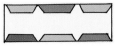

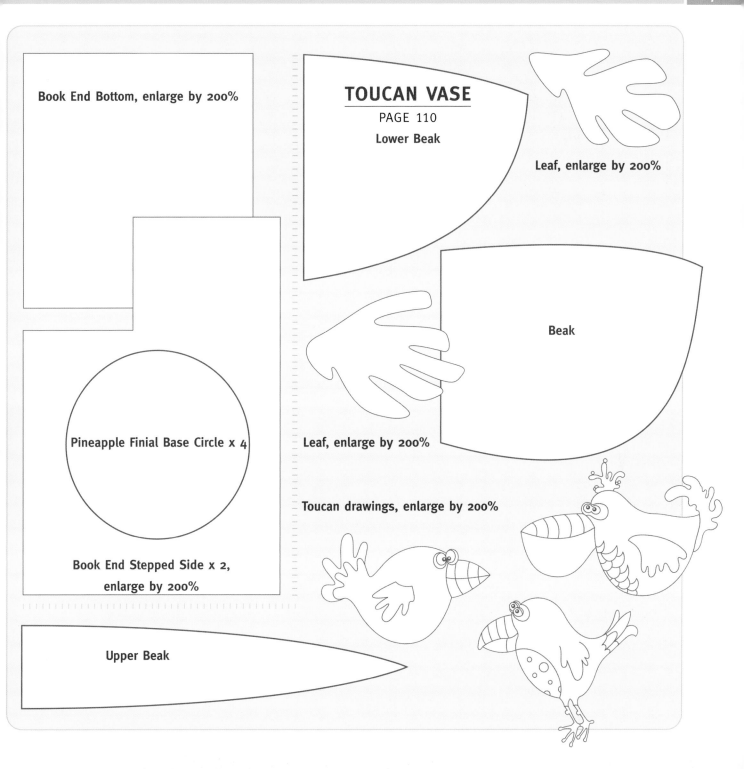

Book End Bottom, enlarge by 200%

TOUCAN VASE
PAGE 110
Lower Beak

Leaf, enlarge by 200%

Beak

Pineapple Finial Base Circle x 4

Leaf, enlarge by 200%

Toucan drawings, enlarge by 200%

Book End Stepped Side x 2,
enlarge by 200%

Upper Beak

INDEX

ACKNOWLEDGMENTS

The author would like to thank Martin Norris for his talent and patience, Michael Brunt for his know how and good humour and Muriel Cochrane for her love.

Breslich & Foss Ltd would like to thank the following individuals for their help in the creation of this book:

Jane Birch for editorial assistance
Stephen Dew for the templates
Elizabeth Healey for design
Janet Ravenscroft for commissioning the book and project management